A CRUISING GUIDE TO
Trinidad and Tobago

OTHER BOOKS BY STEPHEN J. PAVLIDIS:

A Cruising Guide to the Exuma Cays Land and Sea Park; ISBN 0-9638306

The Exuma Guide, A Cruising Guide to the Exuma Cays, 2nd Edition; ISBN 0-9639566-7-1

On and Off the Beaten Path, The Central and Southern Bahamas Guide; ISBN 0-9639566-9-8

The Turks and Caicos Guide, 2nd Edition; ISBN 1-892399-11-3

The Abaco Guide; ISBN 1-892399-02-4

The Puerto Rico Guide; ISBN 1-892399-12-1

More information on these publications and the latest updates are available at www.seaworthy.com
To find out more about the author, visit Steve's Web site at: www.islandhopping.com

A CRUISING GUIDE TO

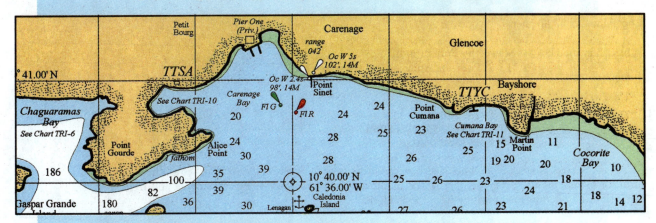

Trinidad and Tobago

Stephen J. Pavlidis

Seaworthy Publications, Inc. • PORT WASHINGTON, WISCONSIN

A Cruising Guide To Trinidad and Tobago
by Stephen J. Pavlidis

Copyright ©2003 Stephen J. Pavlidis

Published in the USA by: **Seaworthy Publications, Inc.**
215 S. Park St., Suite #1
Port Washington, WI 53074
Phone 262-268-9250
Fax 262-268-9208
E-mail custserv@seaworthy.com
Web www.seaworthy.com

All rights reserved. No part of this book may be reproduced stored in a retrieval system, or transmitted in any form, or by any means, electronic, mechanical, photocopying, recording, or by any storage and retrieval system, without permission in writing from the Publisher.

CAUTION: Charts are not to be used for navigational purposes. They are intended as supplements for NOAA, DMA, or British Admiralty charts and no warranties are either expressed or implied as to the usability of the information contained herein. The Author and Publisher take no responsibility for their misuse.

A publication like this is actually the result of a blending of many people's talents, knowledge, and experiences. I would like to take this opportunity to thank the following for their help in this effort: Capt. Lee Bakewell of the S/V *Winterlude* for his help with programming; Eduardo Calcano of the S/V *Cisne*; Jack Dausend, publisher of *The Boca*; Ken and Vesta Douglas of the S/V *Great White Wonder*; Ralph Gibson; Rick Harrison of the S/V *Nosirrah*; Jesse James' *Members Only Maxi-Taxi*; John and Vivian and the staff at *Bluewater Books and Charts* in Ft. Lauderdale; Sandy and Ron Levonson of the S/V *Slow Dance;* Trevor and Ley Liverson of the S/V *Boon;* Gaylord Kelshaw; Melodye and John Pompa of the S/V *Second Millenium*; Joseph Ramnath, the dockmaster at *TTYC*; Norman Sabeney; Jean A. Stampfli, the manager of *TTYC*; Annette and Leslie of *Trump Tours*; Pat Turpin; Jack and Patricia Tyler of the S/V *Whoosh*. If there is anybody that I have neglected to mention here, rest assured that it is an oversight and I sincerely apologize.

Photographs by Author

Library of Congress Cataloging-in-Publication Data

Pavlidis, Stephen J.
 A cruising guide to Trinidad and Tobago / Stephen J. Pavlidis.
  p. cm.
 Includes bibliographical references and index.
 ISBN 1-892399-13-X
  1. Boats and boating--Trinidad and Tobago--Guidebooks. 2. Harbors--Trinidad and Tobago--Guidebooks. 3. Trinidad and Tobago--Guidebooks. I. Title

GV776.29.T75 P38 2002
796.1'0972983--dc21

2002030329

Dedication

Jesse James

Those who have followed my work know that I usually dedicate these books to some of the people that have helped me in my efforts. This time it's a bit different. This book is dedicated to Jesse James, whose unselfish and caring efforts have assisted countless cruisers over the years in Trinidad.

Jesse's *Members Only Maxi-Taxi Service* is well known to cruisers, but most folks don't know that Jesse works long, long hours. He's usually up and gone before dawn, and doesn't get home until almost midnight some nights. His wife, Sharon Rose, must have the patience of Job. However, that's just part of the story.

Besides his usual job of taking cruisers here and there, to the Saturday market, or on a tour to the *Asa Wright Center*, Jesse has been there for cruisers when they needed his help the most. Many times Jesse has gone out of the way to make life easier for cruisers, to help them solve their problems, and Jesse has asked nothing in return, being satisfied in the knowledge that their problems have been solved. In more private moments, Jesse has been there to comfort those in need who had no other family save Jesse's.

Jesse, this one's for you my friend!

Contents

- **INTRODUCTION** 1
- **A BRIEF HISTORY OF TRINIDAD AND TOBAGO** 3
- **THE BASICS** 9
  - Caribbean Etiquette 9
  - Carnival 10
  - Culture 12
  - Currency 13
  - Customs and Immigration 14
  - Diving 15
  - Education 15
  - Ferries 16
  - Flora and Fauna 16
  - Getting Around 18
  - Government 19
  - Ham Radio 19
  - Holidays 20
  - Hurricanes 21
  - Internet in Trinidad and Tobago 22
  - Leaving Your Boat in Trinidad 22
  - Medical Emergencies 23
  - Phoning Home 23
  - Propane 23
  - Provisioning and Shopping 23
  - Security 24
  - Tides and Currents 25
  - Time 26
  - VHF 26
  - Weather 26
  - YSATT 27

- **USING THE CHARTS** 29
- **LIST OF CHARTS** 31
- **INDEX OF CHARTS** 32
  - Trinidad 32
  - Tobago 33
- **TRINIDAD** 34
  - Boca del Dragon 34
    - Monos Island 34
    - Scotland Bay 37
    - Huevos Island 38
    - Chacachacare Island 38
  - The Western Coast of Trinidad 41
    - Chaguaramas 41
    - Facilities Directory, Chaguaramas Bay 41
    - Gaspar Grande 48
    - Five Islands 50
    - Carenage Bay and TTSA 51
    - Cumana Bay and TTYC 52
    - Port of Spain 55
    - Point-a-Pierre 59
    - San Fernando 59
  - The Northern Coast 61
    - La Vache Bay 63
    - Maracas Bay 64
    - Las Cuevas Bay 65
    - Chupara Point 66
  - The Southern and Eastern Coasts ... 68

TOBAGO 71

- Rockly Bay, Scarborough 73
- Crown Point to Pigeon Point 75
- Buccoo Reef and Buccoo Bay 77
- Mt. Irvine Bay 80
- Grafton Bay 81
- Great Courland Bay, Plymouth 82
- Castara Bay 86
- Englishman's Bay 87
- Parlatuvier Bay 88
- Man of War Bay, Charlotteville 90
- The Northeastern Tip, The Melville Islands 93
- Tyrrel's Bay, Speyside 95
- King's Bay 97

LOCAL CUISINE 98

APPENDIX 100

- A: Navigational Lights 100
- B: GPS Waypoints 103
- C: Marinas 105
- D: Service Facilities 105
- E: Logarithmic Speed Scale 110
- F: Depth Conversion Scale 110
- G: Metric Conversion Table 110

REFERENCES AND BIBLIOGRAPHY 111

INDEX 112

ABOUT THE AUTHOR 116

NOTES 117

Introduction

I**T IS OUR DUTY** to proceed from what is near to what is distant, from what is known to what is less known, to gather the traditions from those who have reported them and to leave the rest as it is . . .
Tahqiq ma lil-hind, Abu'l-Rayhan Muhammad al-Biruni, 973–1050

The island of Trinidad has become a major cruising destination for vessels in the Caribbean, and with good reason. Trinidad's marine service industry has blossomed over the last decade, and if you tie that in with the fact that the islands of Trinidad and Tobago are technically out of the hurricane zone (at least the insurance underwriters treat them that way), you have an attractive combination for seasonal visitors.

The island of Trinidad has a strong magnetic quality about her that has become an accepted fact among veteran cruisers, many of whom call these islands home. There are many vessels that initially call at Trinidad planning to stay a week, or a month, and wind up staying many times longer than they had originally planned. The *Immigration* officers know this, and if you don't ask for the maximum stay allowed, they might give it to you anyway. Doing so will save you and them the hassle of an extension when you realize that your stay will be a bit longer than you first imagined, and trust me, that will likely happen. It happened to me and I don't know how many other skippers.

What is the attraction? Well, I've tried, but I can't quite define it. I think that it may be different for each and every person. Some like the haulout facilities so they can leave their boat on the hard while they return home for a visit. Others like the fact that they can get just about anything repaired or fabricated for their boat at a very good price. Some like the shopping, or the camaraderie of hundreds of other cruisers, the get-togethers and pot-lucks that go hand-in-hand with the cruising lifestyle. But, let's not limit ourselves to what is attractive in services and social events. There is a LOT more to Trinidad and Tobago.

First and foremost is what is possibly the greatest party in the world . . . *CARNIVAL!* All else pales in comparison to that colorful, highly energetic celebration of life. The topography of Trinidad ranges from the mountainous tropical rain forests in the north to the rolling hills of the southern island. On both the east and west coasts are huge swamps with a tremendous range of creatures large and small. The *Cocal* along the southeastern shore is not to be missed, miles and miles of coconut trees backing up a beach that stretches for miles. Tobago has its own rain forest along with scenic mountain views and diving and snorkeling opportunities to rival any in the Caribbean. Okay, okay, I'll stop . . .

I'm starting to sound like a tourist publication. Besides, you'll learn about all these things within the pages of this publication. But one of the greatest treasures of these islands, and one that I can't put on paper here, is the endearing quality of the people that reside there. Known far and wide for their simple, open friendliness, Trinidadians, Trinis for short, are welcoming and quick to make one feel at home. They will create many warm memories of your visit here, something to look back on one day and smile about.

Whether you come here for a week, for a month, for a season, or for years, you will one day leave Trinidad, even if just for a while, but Trinidad will never leave you.

STEPHEN J. PAVLIDIS
S/V IV Play
TTYC
Bay Shore, Trinidad,
West Indies

A Brief History of Trinidad and Tobago

CENTURIES BEFORE THE BIRTH OF CHRIST, the first settlers in Trinidad arrived upon her shores making the island the first of the Caribbean islands to be populated, and over the following centuries more and more groups of Amerindians from Venezuela arrived on these shores. Springing from the middle Orinoco around 2100 B.C., they moved downriver to the Guyanas, and then up the West Indies chain. During the past half-century, fresh finds, techniques of dating artifacts, and some heated debate, have refined our cumulative knowledge of these people into a sketchy history extending as far back as 4,000 B.C.

The most famous of these groups were the Arawaks and Caribs, who crossed the waters in their dugout canoes and established villages on the island as they progressed up the island chain towards the Bahamas. The people of southern Trinidad kept close cultural ties with their cousins in Venezuela and traded with people as far south as the Guyana's, while the people of northern Trinidad and Tobago maintained ties with the peoples of the Windward Islands.

Up until the early 1500's, more and more Amerindians came to Trinidad, the island they called *Ieri*, land of the hummingbird. In fact, up until the 19th century Amerindians ventured to Trinidad to trade, walking up the long footpath from the southern shore to the mission at Savanna Grande, which today is called the *Indian Walk* (near Princes Town). By the end of the 15th century, there were some 35,000 people inhabiting the islands ranging from the *Kalina* in Tobago to the *Yao, Nepoio, Shebaio* and *Carinepagoto* tribes on Trinidad. Perhaps I should explain something here. All these peoples are Arawaks. An Arawak is simply an Amerindian who speaks the Arawakan language. They include many tribes from the Lucayans in the Bahamas, to the Tainos in Puerto Rico, the Kalina in Tobago and the Caribs who were to be found on all the islands of the Caribbean. Today, their only relatives are the *Lokono Arawaks* in the Guyanas.

On July 31, 1498, Christopher Columbus "discovered" Trinidad on his third voyage to the New World, saying a prayer as he spied the southern hills of Trinidad in the distance after a long spell at sea with dwindling water rations. Columbus, named the island *La Trinite*, after the *Blessed Trinity* to whom he prayed. Columbus traveled along the southern shore anchoring at Moruga, the entire passage there now being shown as *The Columbus Channel* on some tourist maps (but not on any official charts). Just off the southwestern tip of Trinidad, Columbus was approached by a pirogue full of Amerindians armed with bows and arrows. Columbus ordered music and his sailors to dance so as to entertain the visitors. The Indians mistook this for a war dance and let loose with a volley of arrows to which the Spaniards responded in kind causing the Indians to flee. The next day Columbus headed north, never setting foot on the island of Trinidad. Columbus later sailed by Tobago, which he named *Assumpcion* and Grenada, which he called *Concepcion*.

Shortly thereafter Spanish slavers arrived searching for divers for the pearl beds off Margarita and Cubagua, and began what is little less than genocide. At first the Indians were skeptical about fighting back, they were unsure if a white man could be killed. A *cacique* (chief) named Brayoan had an idea. He and his men found a Spaniard passing through their area and offered to escort him and carry him across a river on their shoulders. Once in deep water the Indians they threw the Spaniard into the water and held him under until he drowned, proving that the white man could indeed be killed. Try as they may, the Indians were unsuccessful in their fight for survival and in a few short years the Spaniards decimated the indigenous population. By 1510, there were declared to be no peaceful Indians on the islands. In 1511, the King of Spain forbade slave trading on the islands of Trinidad and Tobago, but this was reversed sometime around 1532. Today all that remains of these first inhabitants are bits of their language, the names of various places, rivers, and mountains on the islands of Trinidad and Tobago.

For almost three hundred years after Columbus there were no settlers on the island save the Spaniards who used Trinidad as a base for exploring the upper reaches of the Orinoco River. Which was where they believed that *El Dorado*, a mythical city of gold, could be found. Along with the Spaniards came Capuchin monks who tried to convert the Amerindians who were not enslaved and removed from the islands. As you will soon learn, the Spaniards were attacked time and time again over the years. Once by Sir Walter Raleigh, himself on a quest for *El Dorado*, who sacked the town of St. Joseph, the old capital of Trinidad that lay 12 miles east of today's capital, Port of Spain. A later invasion by the Dutch resulted in the Spanish survivors becoming nudists for a while as the invaders took all their possessions, including their clothes.

The Spaniards allotted a number of Amerindians to work on the local plantations where missionaries attempted to convert the Indians to Catholicism. On December 1, 1699, three missionaries were slain by Amerindians at the mission of *San Francisco de los Arenales*. The "peaceful" Indians also killed the Governor and several soldiers who arrived later to restore order. The bodies of the martyrs were brought to the church in St. Joseph's and interred under the floor and the Spaniards gathered their forces and set off after the Indians who had committed the deed. The Indians, pursued by the Spanish, fled across the island to the eastern coast where they committed suicide by leaping off a cliff into the huge breakers at Toco at the northeastern tip of Trinidad. The plantation owners realized that the Missions were not working and they were eventually abolished by 1708, although four remained at Savanna Grande (now Princes Town), Guayria (now Naparima), Savanetta, and Montserrate.

The Spaniards were growing tobacco on the island by this time as the drug had become quite popular in Europe although it was not legal at the time. Dutch and English smugglers moved the illicit drug until a Spanish fleet destroyed all foreign ships in the Gulf of Paria in 1610 (Am I the only one that thinks this whole scenario sounds familiar, an illegal smoking drug, illicit trade, Caribbean based?). American tobacco growers began to dominate the tobacco market so the Trinidadian plantation owners began to grow cocoa until a disease wiped out the cocoa famers in 1725 and a smallpox epidemic further decimated the local population. The remaining Spanish settlers concentrated themselves in St. Joseph until a coup by members of the town council 1745 almost destroyed the settlement. The resident Governor was taken hostage and order was only restored after a Spanish military force from Venezuela arrived. In 1757, the governing body in Trinidad moved from St. Joseph, 12 miles westward to a small fishing village on the coast at *Puerto de Espana*, Port of Spain. Where within two decades the town had grown to about 80 houses, one church, and a battery consisting of several cannons.

At this time Trinidad was still trading with other nations, but foreign settlers were not permitted on the island. However, in 1776, Governor Manuel Flaquez sought to attract Roman Catholic immigrants to Trinidad, particularly French planters, and offered land grants and tax incentives. But was it the planters or their African slaves that were really in demand? These laborers had brought so much already to the islands of Barbados and Haiti, and it is believed that Flaquez was a man of foresight who realized what this labor force could do for Trinidad. Soon, Frenchmen from Grenada, unhappy with their new British rulers, began to trickle into Trinidad. One of them, Roume de St. Laurent, suggested the *Cedula of Population*, which proposed that any European white of the Catholic faith be welcome in Trinidad. In 1783, the King of Spain agreed to the Cedula and between 1783 and 1797, thousands of French settlers and their African slaves arrived in Trinidad and set up vast sugar plantations. Each white settler was granted 130 acres for each member of his family and 65 acres for each slave he brought with him as well as special tax exemptions. There were a few free black settlers who were granted half as much as their white counterparts. The only restrictions were that the settlers had to be Roman Catholic and from a nation on good terms with Spain.

Tobago at this time was going through several changes of leadership over the years, changing Kings 31 times, and currently being ruled by the French. Tobago was originally settled by the British in 1625 when the first group of settlers were wiped out by the indigenous Kalina Indians. In 1628, the Dutch arrived, but a combined force of Indians and Spaniards from Trinidad arrived in canoes and killed off the Dutch settlers. This was the only time that Trinidad and Tobago ever went to war with each other. In 1639, the British arrived again, only to be run off again by the Kalina. Charles I gave the island to his godson the Duke of Courland (in Latvia) and another settlement was established at Plymouth in 1642 by the Courlanders. Again the settlers made like a ping-pong ball being chased off by the Indians, returning in 1650, and again in 1654. At this time the Dutch returned and claimed dominion of the island until they were driven off by the British who were in turn driven off by the French who destroyed the settlements and abandoned the island.

In 1674, Tobago was ceded to the Dutch and the ownership of the islands bounced back and forth between the French, Dutch, Latvian, and English for many years. The United States briefly ruled the island for a period in 1778, just before the French regained possession, which for so many years was no more than a base for pirates. In 1783, in a move to thwart the Spanish government in Trinidad, the French got on the bandwagon and offered a similar immigration policy with large cash compensations to attract French settlers away from the Spanish colony.

Between 1783 and 1797 the population of Trinidad grew from 4,500 to over 16,000 people. This number included slaves, but the Amerindian population declined during the same period from 1,900 to about 1,000. It is estimated that the slaves outnumbered the freemen by a ration of 2 to 1 during these years.

Trinidad had a new governor at this time, Don José Maria Chacon (the national flower, the *Chaconia*, is named after him), who embraced the new colonization policies of the island. The island itself, though under Spanish rule, became increasingly French in flavor and customs with more and more French settlers taking important administrative posts with only one-third of the governing body, the *Cabildo*, being Spanish. The predominant language was French on the streets of Port of Spain, and *Carnival* originated about this time among the planters.

About this time Britain and France were engaged in the Napoleonic Wars which even affected Trinidad, half-a-world away, with British and French warships battling in the Gulf of Paria. In 1796, British sailors from *HMS Alarm*, fresh from sinking French privateers in the Gulf, arrived in Port of Spain and became involved in fighting with some of the French inhabitants of the capital city. Governor Chacon petitioned Madrid for reinforcements and while awaiting help was offered assistance by the French emissary, Victor Hughes. Chacon declined saying that if unsuccessful in his conflict with the British, he would rather the colony fall into the hands of the British than the French settlers. In September of 1796, five Spanish ships under the command of Admiral Ruiz de Apodaca, sailed from Puerto Rico to Trinidad with over 700 soldiers, most of whom immediately were beset with yellow fever. A month later Spain declared war on Britain citing the incident with the *HMS Alarm*.

On February 16, 1797, eighteen British ships under the command of Sir Ralph Abercromby and Sir Henry Harvey, sailed into the Gulf of Paria with the intent of capturing Trinidad. Outnumbered by over 2 to 1, Governor Chacon decided not to offer any opposition to the British fleet. However, not wishing to allow his ships to fall into British hands, Chacon ordered Admiral Apodaca to set fire to the Spanish fleet anchored in Chaguaramas Bay and the Governor surrendered the next day. The terms of surrender were very generous. Chacon's soldiers were allowed to return to Spain, administrative officers were to remain at their posts, and Spanish law was to be maintained. Port of Spain then became the capital of the British colony (and remained the capital until August 31, 1962 when Trinidad and Tobago gained independence), and everybody was required to swear loyalty to the Crown and having done just that, were permitted to keep their property and holdings. Those who still considered themselves as French citizens were given safe conduct off the island to another colony.

After appointing Thomas Picton as governor, Abercromby returned to his fleet and left. Thus beginning Picton's infamous six-year rule. Intimidation, torture, and executions were the rule of Picton's term, and the slaves bore the brunt of his terror. Picton's policies were not inline with British standards as he attempted to foster an illegal trade with Venezuela through Port of Spain. Picton even assisted Venezuelan rebels and eventually the Governor of Cumana placed a bounty of 20,000 pounds on Picton's head . In return, Picton offered a reward of twenty pounds for the head of the Governor of Cumana. In 1801, the Crown praised Picton's zeal, but a year later denounced him as an embarrassment for promoting a slave colony (Britain wanted a free white colony). In 1803, Picton was indicted for torturing a young black girl and the office of Governor of Trinidad was up in the air.

At this same time Tobago changed hands for the last time as the British claimed the island and were backed up by the Congress of Vienna in 1815. Between the British and French, Tobago became a major exporter of sugar and cotton thanks to slave labor. Up until about 1774, Tobago was plagued with almost annual slave revolts until a savage retaliation quelled any thoughts of revolt for the rest of the century. Tobago's population at this time was around 15,000, quite populous for such a small nation when you consider that the much larger Trinidad did not have that many more settlers. A planned slave revolt in 1801 was exposed and some 200 slaves from 16 different plantations arrested. Within two weeks, six rebel leaders were executed (burnt alive), four banished, and the rest flogged and return to their plantations. This quieted slave matters for decades to come.

In 1834, the abolition of slavery brought new problems to the plantation owners. As freed slaves moved off the plantations a new labor force was required. The plantation owners were recompensed for their property losses, and slaves were apprenticed to their former owners for periods of 2–4 years. Slaves protested in Port of Spain, and the militia moved in to calm things down. Until 1837, when some 40 rebels, mutineer members of the *First West Indian Regiment*, lost their lives, their leaders summarily executed in St. Joseph's. By the time the former slave's apprenticeship periods ended early in 1838, the plantation owners required a new labor force. The plantation owners, seeking to maintain a dependable workforce, offered former slaves housing and wages, but most of the slaves left. Many settled in and around the towns and began eking out a living as best they could. Others squatted illegally on lands they could not afford to purchase. The Crown, refusing to distribute Crown Land to those who were landless, could do nothing to prevent squatting. In 1846, the *Sugar Duties Act* allowed cheaper foreign sugar into Crown lands which naturally enraged the sugar planters in Trinidad and Tobago. The sugar economy fell in the islands, many sugar plantations were abandoned (and many new cocoa plantations sprang up), but most survived and recovery was only going to come with a dependable work force. At this time some 3,000 Africans from Sierra Leone arrived in Trinidad, but they eventually abandoned their duties on the sugar plantations. Portuguese from Madeira and Chinese arrived and set up shops on the island. One day in May of 1845, the *Fatel Rozack* docked at Port of Spain with the answer to the plantation owner's woes, 225 immigrants from Calcutta.

India at this time was a British colony with a large destitute population who were used to a tropical climate and agriculture. Unfortunately, the first immigrants soon left the plantations in Trinidad and the answer became apparent; an indentureship contract, just another form of slavery some would later claim. In 1848, the Crown agreed to sponsor the immigration of indentured laborers from India, an act that would have an impact on the economy as well as the future of Trinidad and her culture. By 1851, a steady flow of Indians entering Trinidad began, and continued until 1917 when the Indian government stopped the practice. But by then some 144,000 Indians had arrived in Trinidad, many quarantined on Nelson Island (in the Five Islands area just south of Carenage), Trinidad's version of New York's Ellis Island.

The indentureship agreement bound the workers to the plantation owner for a period of three years. This was followed by a two-year "industrial residence" period during which the worker was permitted to re-indenture to any plantation or find another occupation provided they pay a special "occupation tax". After five years the worker was given what was known as "free paper." If they wanted free passage back to India they had to remain in the colony for another five years. After 1895, indentured workers were required to pay a portion of their return passage. As one would imagine, thousands of East Indian workers stayed in Trinidad after their contracts were fulfilled. Their descendants make up approximately 40% of Trinidad's current population.

At that time Tobago was going through some extremely hard times as the island was bankrupt as of Emancipation Day. Wages were too low to even attract laborers from Barbados, convicts, freed slaves from the Americans, or Africans from Sierra Leone. If that were not enough Mother Nature gave a helping hand by devastating the island's crops in 1847. Tobago was becoming increasingly unattractive to planters as well as workers. And then somebody came up with what's known as the *Meraire System*, whereby workers took no pay, instead sharing in the profits of the crop with the land owner. This oral agreement worked find until the 1870's when the sugar industry declined and planters reneged on their agreements leading to riots by workers. The *Belmanna Riots*, named after a corporal who was sent to arrest the riot's leaders, convinced the planters that the *Metaire System* was not working. Tobagans realized that British rule was preferred to the self-governing, almost feudal system that was currently in effect so in 1877 Tobago became a British Crown Colony. Twenty years later Tobago became a "ward" of Trinidad and united the two islands forever. Soon sugar would fall by the wayside as the prime element in the Trinidadian economy, to be replaced by oil.

The fist oil well in Trinidad was drilled at La Brea in 1857, but it was over half-a-century later when the first oil refinery was constructed at Point-a-Pierre at the beginning of the first World War. Trinidadian soldiers volunteered for active duty and at first were refused until King George intervened. They formed a West Indian contingent that was not a part of the real British Army and received lower pay for simply being black. At this time only whites were eligible for commissions as officers. Though generally kept from combat with Europeans, some units saw action in Egypt against the Turks. After countless instances of racism from their military peers, the disgruntled Trinidadians returned home after the war.

Over the years many oil wells were drilled in the southern areas of Trinidad at Guayaguayare, Palo Seco, Erin, Siparia, Tabaquite, and Rousillac. One of the pioneers of the oil industry was a Brit named Randolph Rust who immigrated to Trinidad in 1881. *There is a small bay named after him on the island of Chacachacare.* Even with the burgeoning oil industry, the post war years brought hardship and high inflation to Trinidad. A dockworker's strike in 1919 almost turned into a national movement for higher wages. And as one would expect, the depression years affected Trinidad as well. Uunemployment rose and those that did have jobs, found shrinking wages and greater workloads. The oil industry was growing but workers were striking for more money and riots seemed to be the order of the day with both strikers and policemen dying as protests turned fatal.

The advent of World War II brought the Americans

to the island nation. In 1940, Great Britain leased to the United States several Crown Lands including the western coast of Trinidad at Chaguaramas for a period of 99 years. In return the Crown received fifty antiquated warships as part of FDR's *Lend-Lease* program.

Trinidad was a hub of Allied and Axis activity due to its strategic location. Over eighty ships were sunk by German U-boats in the waters surrounding Trinidad. Two German U-boats entered Port of Spain and sunk two ships at King's Wharf. Another U-boat entered Chaguaramas Bay and shelled the surrounding shoreline. This activity caused the placement of a steel submarine net stretching from Chacachacare westward north of Patos Island almost to the Venezuela shoreline.

During the war years, the United States stationed over 50,000 troops on Trinidad and within eight years they were for the most part gone, leaving a skeleton crew at the Chaguaramas Naval Base. These years created a boom in employment on Trinidad, and thousands of people found well-paying positions in an economic balloon that was to burst shortly after the war's end. But is was not just the labor force that benefited, land, hotel and home owners received inflated rents, restaurants, garages, taxi drivers, and bars also did a thriving business. All across the island roads and bridges were constructed, large areas of land leveled, and ugly spots transformed into scenes of beauty. In the medical field, Trinidad gained much from American health authorities whose talents, expertise, and knowledge were years in advance of the existing conditions in the prevention, treatment, and cure of disease, as well as hospital administration and supervision.

One benefit turned out to be a double-edged sword. Trinidad gained from the influx of large numbers of workers from Barbados, St. Lucia, Grenada, and St. Vincent, who came to Trinidad seeking employment on the American military bases. However, when the military left, mounting unemployment plagued the islanders that remained, the majority of whom decided to take up permanent residence in Trinidad. Another sad by-product was the racial prejudice the Americans brought with them. In 1945, *Life* magazine reported instances where U.S. military personnel would keep a brown paper bag at the door of their parties. Those that were lighter than the bag were considered "white" and allowed to enter.

But the economic boom was just an upside to a social downside, the family life suffered and few gains were made in education and agriculture during these years, nothing lasting. But one of the greatest gifts the American gave to Trinidad and her people would soon make her people, culture, and musicians, world famous.

The Americans left untold numbers of oil drums behind. Some inventive musicians in the Port of Spain area formed these oil drums into musical instruments that are now symbolic with almost all Caribbean music and it's own form known as *Pan*. *Pan* music also helped to transform *Carnival* into a world class event instead of a local festival, today *Carnival* is known as possibly the greatest party in the world.

On July 4, 1973, Trinidad signed the *Treaty of Chaguaramas* establishing the *Caribbean Community and Common Market, CARICOM*. The treaty was signed in Chaguaramas at an old military barracks that the Trinis rebuilt in six weeks. That barracks was again restored in 1999 and today is known as the *Chaguaramas Hotel and Convention Center*. For the *CARICOM* signing, works of local artists were used to decorate the building. Some of these are still present on the site.

The founding members of *CARICOM* were Barbados, Guyana, Jamaica, and Trinidad and Tobago. Over the years Belize, Dominica, Grenada, St. Lucia, St. Vincent and the Grenadines, Monteserrat, Antigua, St. Kitts, Nevis, and Anguilla joined in. The Bahamas signed on also, but is not a member of the *Common Market*. The BVI and the Turks and Caicos are *Associate Members* and Haiti is a *Provisional Member*.

On August 1, 1976, Trinidad and Tobago became an independent republic and the 70's saw an economic boom in Trinidad with rising oil prices the world over. The 1980's however turned out just the opposite as oil prices fell worldwide.

Today Trinidad and Tobago are seeing an increase in the tourism industry that along with the strong petroleum industry offers a bright future to the dual-island nation.

The Basics

To BEGIN WITH, let me suggest that upon arrival in Chaguaramas, you pick up a free copy of the *Trinidad/Tobago Boater's Directory*. This helpful publication is available at all marinas, *YSATT*, and most of the marine chandlers. There is a wealth of information here including daily tide tables as well as an up-to-date listing of marine services available.

CARIBBEAN ETIQUETTE

Proper etiquette is important when visiting foreign lands; lack of it can be embarrassing at the least and can create serious misunderstandings. For instance, when greeting people as you board a bus, give a hearty "Good morning" (if indeed it is morning) all around and it will be returned. The rule is greetings first, business later. Not offering a greeting first may be perceived as rude. If you approach a home that has a fence, stop at the front gate and say loudly "Inside." If you receive no answer, try again. If there is still no answer, the folks are either not at home or don't wish to be disturbed.

And while we're talking about talking here, let's touch upon the words that will grace your ears in Trinidad. Many cruisers have problems understanding the Trinis at times. They look questionably with wide eyes as someone speaks and wonder "What language do they speak here?" Well, they speak English here, the same as most of us do. Correction, not quite the same. At one end of the spectrum is standard English, at the other end is Caribbean Creole, which differs from standard English in syntax, and a Trini may speak anywhere between the two. Generally, when speaking standard English, it is spoken a bit faster and the words sometimes shortened and corrupted to the point where *downtown* comes out as *dunton*, and *gone* is *gorn*. Don' panic mon', you'll get the hang of it. I wish I had a dollar for every time that I've had to ask a Trini to please repeat what he or she said as I couldn't understand a word since the first word passed their lips. Oddly enough, if you listen long enough, you'll notice differences between Tobago Creole and Trinidadian Creole. Experts say that the Tobagan Creole is more akin to the Jamaican Creole.

You'll probably notice a lot of French influence in the language, a bit different from places in the northern Caribbean such as Nevis where there is a bit more of a Portuguese influence. There is also a considerable French and Hindu influence that extends to everyday language in the names of things and places. The words you hear in Trinidad and Tobago will fall upon your ears as strange at first until you realize where they come from and what they describe. Yes it is English spoken here, with a colorful and rich infusion of other tongues as well.

And by the way, when two people are speaking, as with good manners everywhere, it is extremely rude to interrupt. West Indians don't do it, neither should you.

Many Americans judge a man by the grip of his handshake, this does not work in the Caribbean where a soft, gentle hand "embrace" is more the norm. I've head some folks (Canadians and Americans, never the British) say that they are surprised that West Indians do not smile. This can create the misconception that the person does not like the cruiser. This is, to say the least, ridiculous. West Indian manners call for a reserved face to be shown, saving the smile for something funny or someone they are familiar with. The lack of a smiley-face should not imply a negative attitude to the visitor unaccustomed to the lifestyle here in the Caribbean.

Finally, let's discuss a very important subject, it will be a part of a lot that you do here in Trinidad and Tobago. Let's take a moment and touch briefly upon the Caribbean pastime of *liming*. If you're invited to join a group for a drink or a bite to eat, by all means, do! Hang out! You'll be *liming*! People in the Caribbean can be found *liming* everywhere, in the streets, in restaurants and bars, at home, or even on your boat. *Liming* is just chilling, hanging out . . . get the picture?

CARNIVAL

Yes, this is it! If you come to Trinidad for no other reason, it should be to experience *Carnival*. Do you like a parade? Do you like a party? If you do, you'll love Trinidad as the entire island focuses on parades and parties the week of *Carnival* and the six weeks leading up to it. This is it, *Carnival*, the big one, the biggest party of them all.

I can only touch upon the basics of *Carnival* here, but cruisers in Trinidad wanting to learn more about *Carnival* are in luck. For over 8 years now, Jack Dausend, publisher of *The Boca*, has been putting on the *"Taste of Carnival"* seminars in Chaguaramas. These seminars are geared toward educating the visiting cruiser about *Carnival* and assisting them to become participants instead of observers. Jack's works have met with great success and are a definite "must-do" when in Trinidad. Check with Jack in his office at *Crews Inn* (next to *Immigration*), or listen to the daily VHF net for times and places. You can also check the section on Internet access later in this chapter for some interesting *Carnival* related websites. Your best bet for finding information on what events are occurring and where, is to read the local newspapers, *The Guardian*, or *Newsday*, for the latest *Carnival* schedules. Most of the festivities are centered in Port of Spain and to a lesser extent in San Fernando, Arima, and other towns all over the island nation. Cruisers and their vessels can get in the *Carnival* spirit together in the *Carnival Fun Race* sponsored by the good folks at *TTSA* at the Carenage. Choose a *Carnival* theme and decorate your boat and crew accordingly, the more outrageous concept the better, and enter the race and join the party. After the race prizes are given for the best costume, both local and cruiser, and there is live entertainment and a healthy dose of favorite beverages (all boats entering receive a bottle of the sponsor's rum). For more information check with *TTSA*.

A mixture of French and African celebrations, *Carnival* season actually begins on Boxing Day, the day after Christmas, and the momentum and excitement builds to a crescendo ending at midnight on *Carnival* Tuesday, the eve of Ash Wednesday, the first day of Lent. Trinidadians from all over the world return to their homeland at this time to engage in the fete will all their kinfolk, friends, and neighbors and, yes, even the cruisers are invited to *mas*, to don a costume and join the throngs parading through the streets. *Carnival* is not a show put on for tourists, it is a participatory event. You should be thrilled to take part and interact, it will be an event, and a period of your life, that you will never forget. And *Carnival* is not just for adults, everywhere you go you will see children parading in their own *Carnival* costumes with each school being represented and Saturday activities geared towards the youth of Trinidad.

Some trace *Carnival* (*carne vale-farewell to the flesh*) back to roots in the *Bacchanals* of ancient Greece, others to the Roman fetes of *Saturnalia*.

But one cannot put aside the timing of *Carnival* which is Christian in tone, being a prelude to the weeks of Lent's abstinence. *Carnival* was initially a festival of white French plantation owners in the late 1700's. During the few days before Ash Wednesday, the Creole establishment would invert their roles taking on the guise of field laborers and slaves. The slaves too celebrated *Carnival*, but in secret, until their emancipation in 1834 when they took it to the streets of Port of Spain mimicking and satirizing the colonial gentry. The characters created then are still alive today and *Viey La Cou* (*old yard*) is an organization dedicated to keeping the old traditions and characters alive by utilizing the "yard" at Queen's Hall as a performance spot.

In the first few years after Emancipation, the freed slaves had protection at *Carnival* time, *batonniers*, or *stickmen*, who carried bamboo sticks similar to what was used in the cane fields to put out fires. Today, stickfighting is still one of the many faces of *Carnival* and you'll still see many characters from folklore as well as satirized locals personalities. You'll meet *Midnight Robbers* whose orations are designed to intimidate you into parting with some money, devils called *Jab Jabs*, clowns called *Pierrot Grenade*, human donkeys called *Burrokeets*, giants on stilts called *Moko Jumbies*, *Dame Lorraines*, caricatures of Creole plantation wives, *Jammette's*, the local prostitutes (no they are not prostitutes, they are playing a character), *Jamets*, the "sweet men" or kept lovers, and the cross-dressing *Pisenlets*. The lewd actions of the early characterizations did not sit well with the powers to be. An effort to crackdown on the sexual nature of *Carnival* resulted in a riot in 1881. But *Carnival* was not to be subdued, and a toned down version appeared over the next few years. In the 1890's a music competition was introduced and in the 20th century more and more aspects of *Carnival* became competitions. World War II brought a temporary cessation to *Carnival*, but when the celebration returned, it arrived with a new sound...*Pan*. The original pan drums were made from old 55-gallon oil drums left behind by the U.S. military and were hammered into musical instruments. Today *Pan* music is a worldwide phenomenon and with *Calypso* has become the score for *Carnival*.

Between Christmas and Ash Wednesday, as if you won't have enough to do learning about *Carnival*, making a costume, and attending Jack's seminars, you will likely find yourself caught up in an ocean of fetes. Fetes are parties, some private, some quite public, some free, some quite costly, either way, you will have FUN! Fetes are get-togethers where you can *Lime* (Lime you ask? Read the section on *Culture*.) with the best, eating and drinking (some ticket prices are all-inclusive and the proceeds of some may go to charity) and listening to live bands or a DJ playing the best in *Calypso, Soca,* and *Rapso*. Most fetes sell out early, most are outdoors, and some can get quite rowdy. Either way, *Carnival* without attending a fete will be lacking my friends.

Speaking of lacking, what would *Carnival* be without *Calypso*? *Calypso* songs parody the issues and events of the day and the *Calypso* poet has open license to offer satirical, scathing, and sometimes risqué commentaries that will leave audiences laughing uproariously. Competition between Calypsonians is fierce and throughout the *Carnival* season you'll find the top Calypsonians showcasing their talents nightly in *Calypso Tents*. The *Calypso Tents* are showcases for these performers and the audiences eagerly await their performances. A performer may engage in *Extempo*, an ad-lib event in which he or she must compose and perform a *Calypso* song off the top of their head on a suggested topic. Sometimes two Calypsonians will trade verses back and forth, quite often insulting and always extremely funny, each trying to outdo the other in an event called *Picong*. Don't forget to buy your tickets early for one of the *Calypso* tent festivities and remember that some events may offer a *Ladies Night* with two for one admissions. There are often amateur and junior *Calypso* competitions around the island at this time that are also fun to attend and can be just as entertaining as the pros and the adults. Now let's discuss what else is going on during *Carnival*

Panorama is a nation-wide steelband competition featuring some large pan bands with upwards of 100 musicians. Regional competitions are held and the finals are held at the *Savanna*, the park in Port of Spain. Here you can buy a ticket and find your spot in the grandstands (bring a cooler and a cushion for comfort) and sit back and watch people and listen to *Pan* music. The grandstands themselves are as much a show as the performers, each area being one huge party.

Dimanche Gras, (*Fat Sunday*), is held on the Sunday night before *J'Ouvert*. The show features the King and Queen of the *Band Final Competition*, performances by the Panorama champions, as well as the Extempo winners and the Junior Monarch. Between acts the show does not stall as other performers show their talents while the next act is preparing. This show usually lasts until 0200, the beginning of *J'Ouvert*.

J'Ouvert, pronounced *joo-vay* means *daybreak* in French, is the official start of *Carnival* and is the one event you MUST NOT MISS! To begin with, let me warn you, if you plan to attend *J'Ouvert*, don't wear white, or anything you cannot afford to get dirty, muddy, and wet. All night long, revelers in homemade costumes, will dance in the streets till dawn. Mud and paint rule, and if you're clean, prepare yourself for a hug from a person covered with mud from head to toe. Better to simply jump right in and enjoy, you can always wash off in the morning...if you're not covered in mud, you haven't experienced *J'Ouvert*.

Mas, or *playing mas*, is what the costumed revelers are doing during *Carnival*, either playing their chosen character, or themselves, and you too are invited to *play mas*. First you'll need to register with a *mas* camp and purchase a costume. Today's costumes tend toward the *bikini mas*, generally a bikini style with sequins, feathers, and whatever other creative notions occurs to the costume maker. Remember, you'll be partying in the tropical heat, best to wear as little as possible. The Woodbrook area of Port of Spain is home to numerous *mas camps* and is a hotbed of *pre-Carnival* activity starting as early as November. One of the most popular of the *mas* groups is Peter Minshalls *Callaloo mas camp,* now in Chaguaramas (see Peter's website at www.callaloo.co.tt), where you can register to play with Peter's group, numbering around 3,000 festive masqueraders. Peter designs the group's costumes and one will set you back about TT$800 and up. To his credit, Peter helped design and choreograph the festivities at the 1992 *Olympics* in Barcelona.

On *Carnival* Monday, *Pretty Mas* begins with its costumed bands and lasts well into the night. Today the bands take to the streets giving you a sample of what you can expect on *Carnival* Tuesday, the climax of the celebrations with the *Parade of Bands*. Tuesday, beginning early in the morning, bands of costumed revelers march past the judging booths and break down into sections, each section with its own particular costume theme. The band with the most energy, spirit, and visual impact wins the prestigious *Band of the Year* competition. The focus of this last event is Queens Park Savanna in Port of Spain and is the one event that most people attend.

There are several things you'll need to know when attending *Carnival*, I will mention a few here, and Jack will give you the details when you attend his seminars. First off, *Carnival*, although not a public holiday, will find many businesses closed so bear that in mind. Make sure you have plenty of TT's (Trinidad/Tobago dollars), and keep your money in your shoe, don't carry a wallet or wear any jewelry, *Carnival* really brings out the pickpockets. And speaking of shoes, make sure they're comfortable as you'll be in them for a long time, especially if you join a parade. Don't take a drink from somebody you don't know, and either bring your own food or buy from vendors with proper food badges. Stay with your friends, there is strength in numbers. If you have to wander off to relieve yourself, don't go alone. And don't try too hard to have fun, it is possible to have TOO much fun; pace yourself, especially if you're not used to staying up long hours and partying hard.

CULTURE

Trinidad/Tobago is a polyglot of cultures, the most diverse spectrum of people in the entire Caribbean. The population of the islands is a melting pot made up primarily of the descendants of freed slaves and the indentured East Indians that replaced them. The population of 1.3 million people is fairly evenly divided between those of

African and East Indian descent, each about 40%, while approximately 18% is of mixed descent, the remainder of the population is made up of Chinese, Arabic, Spanish, and other nationalities.

Nowhere is this mix of cultures more apparent than in downtown Port of Spain, Trinidad. Here you'll find the *Savanna*, a huge park that is the center of *Carnival* activities. Surrounding the park you'll find everything from a U.S. staple (*TGI Friday's*) across the street from a Victorian mansion that sits majestically next a building that you would swear resembles a Moroccan palace. Farther outside of town, you might see a Hindu temple on one corner and just down the road a Mosque sitting across the street from a Catholic Church.

Trinidad is the richest West Indian island in her culture, peoples, and economy. It is the home of the Limbo, steelbands, *Calypso* and *Pan* music, Angostura Bitters, and the roti. The islands are also home to several strange characters. *La Diablesse*, who is often depicted dressed in the rich style of a wealthy Creole woman of the French Antilles. She is characterized by a large hat that conceals her features, a long, rustling petticoat and clinking chain. She is a devil woman and the only way she can be recognized is by her feet, one of which is a hoof. *La Diablesse* is said to be the avenger of wrongdoing against women and works here evil by luring men into the forest to kill them or leave them insane forever and she can only be foiled by wearing one's clothes inside out.

One man who *La Diablesse* has no effect upon is *Papa Bois*, the old man of the forest. *Papa Bois* is the protector of trees and animals and it is his duty to punish those who needlessly kill or harm. It is said that if you meet him, never look at his feet and be extremely polite saying: "Bonjour vieux papal."

Strangest of all perhaps is the *Soucouyant*, an old woman who lives at the outskirts of the village. At night the *Soucouyant* removes her old, wrinkled skin and places it in a mortar jar to prowl the night as a fireball, seeking victims whose lifeblood she can suck out. The only way to destroy her is to place coarse salt in the jar with her skin so she cannot don it again and she finally dies with the coming of dawn.

CURRENCY

The local currency is the Trinidad-Tobago Dollar, or simply, the TT. Paper currency comes in denominations of $1, $5, $10, $20, and $100 (a "blue one"), while coins come in 1¢, 5¢, 10¢, 25¢, and 50¢ pieces. At the time of this writing in the fall of 2002, the current exchange rate was about TT$6.09 to US$1.

ATM's are happy to spew out TT's for you, and there's even a machine at the *Westmoorings Mall* in Port of Spain that will give you U.S. dollars. Although the TT is the official currency in Trinidad and Tobago, many businesses will accept U.S. dollars for payment . . . check first however. Also, if you're ever unsure as to whether or not you've been quoted a price in TT$ or US$, ask!

Trinidad/Tobago adds on a *VAT* (Value Added Tax) of 15% on all goods and services except those marine services (and materials) relating to yachts in transit. Materials purchased not in relation to a service will not be *VAT* free. For instance, if you contract *Power Boats* to paint your bottom, there will be no *VAT* on the paint or the labor. However, if you walk up to *Budget Marine* and purchase a gallon of bottom paint, you will have to pay the *VAT*, but if *Power Boats* then applies the paint, there will still be no *VAT* on the service. Although you may not notice it on a receipt, rest assured that the *VAT* has been collected. If a merchant offers a "*VAT* Free" item, it simply means that the merchant is giving you a 15% discount on the goods and that the item is NOT "*VAT* Free."

Hotels always include a 10% service charge as well as a 10% Hotel Room Tax. If leaving by plane a Departure Tax of TT$100 (must be paid in TT's) will be assessed.

Trinidad and Tobago has the most diversified and industrialized economy in the English speaking Caribbean. Trinidad has a wealth of natural resources, large reserves of oil and natural gas that have contributed greatly to the *Gross National Product*. High oil prices in the 1970's created boom years in the economy of Trinidad and much of the nation's infrastructure was developed in this decade. On the downside, a period of depressed oil prices couple with extremely high levels of public expenditure created a dwindling economy between 1988 and 1993. Today however, under the supervision of the *World Bank* and *IMF*, the economy of Trinidad is back on line and the TT is actually gaining on the U.S. dollar.

CUSTOMS AND IMMIGRATION

Vessels are required to clear with *Customs* and *Immigration* immediately upon arriving in the waters of Trinidad and Tobago. This is a very simple process as there are only a few Ports of Entry in this dual island nation. Nearly all cruisers arriving in Trinidad clear at Chaguaramas and this is recommended. There is a *Customs* office in Port of Spain, as well as Point-a-Pierre. They are both primarily commercial ports and Port of Spain may recommend that you clear at Chaguaramas. Vessels arriving in Tobago now have an alternative to clearing in at Scarborough. As of August 1, 2001, a *Customs* officer was assigned to Charlotteville so you can now clear there. Until now, you could only anchor at Charlotteville and take a bus to Scarborough to clear. As of this writing the *Customs* officer was working out of an office near the Police station just up the road from the dock. In Scarborough, *Customs* is located just to the right of the ferry terminal (east of the terminal) on the 2nd floor of the red-roofed building across from the pizza parlor. *Immigration* is located across the street from the ferry terminal on the 3rd floor of the *NIB* mall by *KFC*.

Although *Customs* and *Immigration* are open 24 hours a day, their normal working hours are 0800-1600 Monday through Friday (except holidays) and arriving outside of these hours will cost you an overtime charge of approximately TT$45.

In Chaguaramas you must proceed directly to the *Customs Dock* (see *Facilities Directory, Chaguaramas Bay* for its location), just past the *Crews Inn Marina* docks (you MUST tie up at this dock unless you wish to pay a hefty fine). Vessels are not permitted to anchor or visit any other area before clearing in at the dock. After your vessel is secure, head down the dock and go between the docked boats and the building on your left that houses *Hi-Lo Market*, *The Lighthouse Restaurant*, and *The Mariners Office*. At the corner walk up the steps, and then climb the stairway to the second floor of the building on your immediate left, this is the *Immigration* office where you must clear first. *Immigration* will want to see all crewmembers upon arrival and departure. All persons visiting Trinidad and Tobago are required to have visas upon entry. However, because of historical ties and bilateral agreements, citizens of several countries are not required to have visas for entry. Citizens of the following countries are not required to have visas for entry: citizens of the U.S.A on vacation for 3 months or less; citizens of Venezuela arriving from Venezuela on vacation for 14 days or less; citizens of Suriname, Martinique, Guadeloupe, French Guyana, Curacao, Aruba, Bonaire, St. Eustatius, St Maarten, Saba, England, Greece, Ireland, Spain, France, Portugal, Italy, Germany, Belgium, Netherlands, Denmark, Luxembourg, Turkey, Sweden (3 months or less), Norway, Austria, Iceland, Finland, Israel, Brazil, Switzerland, Liechtenstein, Columbia, and all Commonwealth countries except Australia, India, New Zealand, Nigeria, Papua New Guinea, Sri Lanka, Tanzania, and Uganda. Citizens of South Africa are allowed entry into Trinidad and Tobago for religious, cultural, sporting, and educational activities with visas issued without reference. For any other purpose applications for visas must be tendered.

As anywhere, ask for the maximum amount of time that you can stay, just in case. So many people come to Trinidad planning only to stay a week, perhaps two, or even a month, and wind up staying three months and then getting another extension for even longer. The length of your stay is completely in the hands of the *Immigration* officer on duty. Ask for three months starting out. Extensions are available for three months to one year and cost a minimum of TT$100. Crewmembers wishing to transfer from one vessel to another may do so provided the crewmember signs off the vessel he arrived on and signs on to the vessel he is leaving aboard. Crew cannot sign on to a vessel that is staying longer than the vessel on which he or she arrived.

When you are finished with *Immigration* head

back down the steps and about 50' to your right is the *Customs* building. Here you will be required to hand over all firearms for the duration of your stay and you will have to show current vaccination records for all dogs and cats (and they will be quarantined aboard your vessel for the duration of your stay).

To have items shipped to you in Chaguaramas you can send them to you at the following address: Yacht In Transit, your boat name, captain's name, Marina (if applicable), Chaguaramas Terminal Point Gourde, Trinidad, West Indies. When your package arrives you must pick it up at the *Customs* office and present your passport and boat papers including your inward clearance. Downstairs at the *Customs* office is their storage room for packages arriving for cruisers and it is packed with packages dating back several years! Please, when you expect your package to arrive, check with *Customs* and pick it up promptly. If you are picking up items at the airport, check with *Customs* before heading to the airport. After picking up the package you must take the item directly to the Chaguaramas *Customs* office, you are not permitted to visit your vessel first. If you are confused as to what constitutes a duty-free yacht part, check with *Customs* first.

This next part is VERY IMPORTANT! If you have cleared into either Trinidad or Tobago, and expect to visit the other island and clear out from there, you must go to *Customs* and *Immigration* and collect your papers to present to *Customs* and *Immigration* on the other island upon arrival. Your papers will be held until you clear out.

DIVING

Diving in the Trinidad and Tobago area is concentrated in Tobago, but that's not to say that there is NO diving in Trinidad. There are two quality dive operations in Chaguaramas and one in Port of Spain. Diving in Trinidad is concentrated in the waters off the northern coast where, although there are no true tropical coral reefs to speak of due to the runoff from the Orinoco River delta, however there is one coral reef, *Salybia Reef* at the northeastern tip of Trinidad near a place called, appropriately enough, *Reefs Point*. But divers should not despair, there are several rock wall dives with huge boulders and crevasses to explore. There are also two wrecks that most dive shops visit, and one or two more that are far more difficult to discern from the surrounding bottom as there is very little left. Diving on the western shore of Trinidad is dependent on the visibility, which is clouded by the runoff from the Orinoco which can vary seasonally.

Diving in Tobago is nothing less than inspiring, enriching for body as well as soul. Most of Tobago's dive sites are enhanced by the nutrient-rich waters of the northward flowing *Guyana Current*, which contributes, by way of the food chain, to dive sites abundant in marine life. All the coral reefs off Tobago, in general, are what are known as fringing reefs, and allow easy access to the shallower parts for snorkeling from the shore.

Deep water dives are centered in the Speyside area around Little Tobago Island and Goat Island, off the north coast at the Sisters, London Bridge, Mt. Irvine Bay (60' wall dive), Great Courland Bay, Arnos Vale, Culloden Bay, and off the southwestern tip of Tobago at Crown Point. Shallow-water reefs are well represented in the popular 4-acre Buccoo Reef, a favorite with snorkelers and glass-bottom boat operators (although this reef appears to be dying). Just northeast of Buccoo Reef is Mt. Irvine Bay where you can dive the wreck of the *Maverick*.

Tank refills are easy in Tobago, there are numerous dive operations on the island willing to help. In Chaguaramas try *Rick's Dive Center* at *Tardieu Marine*, *Hull Support* at *Power Boats*, or at *Coastal Diving Services, Ltd.* at *Tropical Marine*.

EDUCATION

The people of Trinidad and Tobago are well-educated with an adult literacy rate of between 80–85%. Primary level education is mandatory. Approximately 70% of the 12–15 year old age group attending secondary school while the rest pursue other forms of training (approximately 5,000 students attend the 15 vocational and training schools). The Trinidad and Tobago government sponsors a *Youth Training and Employment*

Partnership Programme (YTEPP), where some 8,000 students per year graduate from a 9-month course.

As far as higher education, Trinidad and Tobago is not found lacking here. The *University of the West Indies (UWI)* has one of its campuses at St. Augustine, Trinidad. The university offers undergraduate and post-graduate programs in the areas of agriculture, business administration, engineering, humanities, languages, law, and natural and social sciences to some 3,300 students. The *UWI Institute of Business*, which opened just a few years ago, offers post-graduate courses on business-related topics and develops in-house programs for local companies.

The *National Institute of Higher Education, Research and Technology, (NIHERST)*, operates a college of health science, a college of nursing, a school of languages and an information technology college. The institute is also running a *UNIDO* funded project to develop software-writing skills.

The *Eric Williams Medical Sciences Complex*, located at Mount Hope, between the *Piarco Airport* and Port-of-Spain, is one of the leading facilities of its kind in the Caribbean. The 70+ building complex is both a teaching and medical science facility.

FERRIES

Trinidad and Tobago are connected by a regular ferry so, if you don't feel like beating to windward to visit Tobago, you can hope the ferry for a 5½ hour trip. The ferry costs TT$60 per person for a round trip ticket. Cabins, when available, are TT$180 round trip. You can even bring a car with you at a cost of around TT$200 for a small car on a one-way trip. You need to make car reservations two weeks in advance.

If you are taking the ferry from Port of Spain, be sure to arrive there at least two hours before sailing, and be prepared for a crowd. It is best to book tickets well in advance as they are often sold out, especially the cabins. Once aboard you can relax in chairs on deck or hang out in the bar or restaurant. For more information call the *Port Authority Ferry Services* in Port of Spain, Trinidad at 625-4306, and in Scarborough, Tobago, at 639-2416. The ferry departs from Port of Spain M-F, at 1400, and from Scarborough at 2300. On Sundays the ferry departs Port of Spain at 1100 and Scarborough at 2300.

There is also a passenger and cargo ferry that travels regularly between Port of Spain and Isla Margarita, Guiria, St. Vincent, Barbados, and St. Lucia. For information call the *Global Steamship Agency* at 625-2547. Another suggestion is to speak to Annette or Leslie at *Trump Tours* located at *Crews Inn Marina*.

FLORA AND FAUNA

At one time, over 10,000 years ago, Trinidad and Tobago were a part of the South American continent. As the earth's forces heaved and churned beneath the sea, a mountainous chunk of land was torn from the continent and Trinidad and Tobago were formed. The fauna and flora on these new islands were the same as those found on the mainland of South America, separated by a small body of water just a few miles wide. Today little has changed in this regard, the plants and animals to be found in Trinidad and Tobago are little different from their mainland cousins giving the islands a diversity of fauna and flora disproportionate to their size.

Habitats on the islands include tropical rain forests, savannas, semi-deciduous forest, mangrove swamps and marsh lands. Tobago's rain forest is the oldest protected rain forest in the Western Hemisphere. Tobago's western end is alive with marshes and its northeastern end and offshore islands are bird sanctuaries. On its eastern coast, Trinidad boasts the *Nariva Swamp*, home to the maniteel, a cousin to the Florida manatee, as well as large water snakes, caimans, various parrots, ducks, and many species of fish and birdlife. It has been said that large crocodiles have even turned up here after crossing the Gulf of Paria and being washed down the Orinoco in a flood. The western shore of Trinidad, just south of Port of Spain, is home to the *Caroni Swamp* where tour operators will happily take you to view the beautiful *Scarlet Ibis*, the national bird of Trinidad.

Of all the flora to be found on the islands, you must become aware of one in particular, the *Manchineel Tree*. This tree is very toxic, even its sap, don't stand under one when it's raining, better to get soaking wet. The *Manchineel* can grow to over 40' and resembles an apple tree with green fruit and flowers.

Of course, the prolific mangrove will be found in many places along the shore, as will the seagrape and Indian almond tree with its symmetrical branches. Its nuts can be eaten after they turn brown, but don't expect them to taste like the almond with which you are familiar. Of course palm trees are numerous, especially in the *Cocal*, an old coconut plantation that stretches for miles along the eastern shore of Trinidad from Guayaguayare to Manzanilla.

All over the islands you are likely to run across bromeliads, orchids, and over 2300 varieties of flowering plants. The most colorful are the hibiscus, bougainvillea, torch ginger, the ginger lilly, 40 vividly colored varieties of balisier, and the colorful bird of paradise, a blue and purple flower that resembles a bird's head.

In addition to possessing the flora and fauna of South America, these islands are also influenced by their geographic location, being a perfect stopping point for Northern or Southern migratory birds, butterflies or anything drifting in the ocean or wind currents. Over 430 species of birds, and over 600 species of butterflies have been recorded in Trinidad and Tobago. Of these, 250 species of birds breed in Trinidad and Tobago while over 150 species migrate here on an annual basis from North and South America. I have already mentioned the Scarlet Ibis, but Tobago has its own national bird, the *Cocorico*, a pheasant that is often viewed as little more than vermin. You're also likely to spot any of a number of parrots, toucans, egrets, peregrine falcons, hawks, tanagers, boobies, pelicans, frigate birds, bananaquits, and the most prolific of them all, and usually seen around Chaguaramas and *TTSA*, the vulture. One of the most unusual of TT avian species are the oilbirds. These birds are nocturnal, feeding primarily on fruit. Eating the fruits whole, during flight they regurgitate the seeds helping with the reforestation of Trinidad. With a wingspan of over 3', and a loud, raucous call, they are an impressive sight at night. Their young have high fat content and the Amerindians and Capuchin monks would boil them down for their oil, hence their name. One of the eight known colonies of these birds on Trinidad is on Huevos Island in the Bocas.

Mammals are represented on Trinidad and Tobago by over 100 species, including armadillos, deer, wild hogs, silky anteaters, ocelots, capuchin monkeys, otters, West Indian manatee, and the one species that you will most likely encounter, especially if anchored at Scotland Bay, the howler monkey. You'll know them when you hear them, they roar like lions, especially after a rain. Fewer today, in the last decade they were stricken with a disease that killed off over 90% of the howler monkey population. Another mammal that you'll encounter, and most likely in the same anchorage, is the fruit bat. These can be quite the pest when they fly into your boat at night to dine on fruit left in the open (and leave layers of guano in their wake). The way to combat them is to keep screens in place at night and keep a light shining in the cockpit, though this is not necessarily a guarantee to keep them away. Anchored at *TTSA*, at night you can see the bats in the early evening crossing the road to dine for the night

Reptiles, especially the dangerous ones, are rarely seen except well off the beaten path. Trinidad is home to over 45 different snakes including the boa constrictor, the anaconda (usually only seen deep in the swamps), two small coral snakes, and two highly poisonous snakes, the Fer de Lance, and the Bushmaster, sometimes called the puff adder. Both of these really don't pose a danger to the cruiser unless you take to hiking inland, in the forests and swamps of the island. There are many varieties of lizards from small anoles all the way up to large iguanas. One of the most interesting is the 3' long, brown matte lizard. This speedy lizard will raise itself up on its hind legs and can accelerate from 0–10 mph in 2 seconds. In the swamps and rivers you might come across a caiman, a small, about 3' long, relative of an alligator with an elongated, pointed snout.

The waters of Trinidad and Tobago are fed by

the confluence of the *Equatorial Current* and the freshwater of the Orinoco River and are teeming with many varieties of sea-life. Some of the largest lobster I've ever seen, and I have seen a lot of them during my tenure as a volunteer Asst. Warden at Exuma Park, were on the southeastern shore of Trinidad. Here you might see a roadside stand with live lobster hanging up going for about TT$40.

One final note on sea creatures that will have an immediate effect upon your vessels. First and foremost are the small jellyfish, especially in Chaguaramas that love to block off the water flow to your air-conditioner. The jellyfish are not always around, usually from Easter until June or July, so you get some relief in that regard. *TTYC* does not suffer from the problem as much, though you might see a lot of jellyfish as you approach *TTYC*, inside the jetty the numbers of creatures are far less than what you will experience in Chaguaramas Bay. Another creature you'll have to deal with is the barnacle. These are fertile waters and barnacles are plentiful. Even if you have new bottom paint, if you're sitting at a marina with your air-conditioner running, over a period of time, within six weeks or so, they'll build up inside your intake, seacock, and strainer to immense proportions, diminishing your water flow to almost nothing. There's nothing I know of to stop their attack, perhaps you have a secret you can share, I'd love to know it. Maintenance and a periodic cleaning of the system, is probably the best preventative.

GETTING AROUND

Getting around in Trinidad and Tobago is not difficult. There are several car rental companies if you are so inclined. Cruisers that possess a valid driver's license issued in the U.S., Canada, France, U.K., Germany, and the Bahamas, may drive for up to three months (of course, international licenses are also accepted).

Driving is on the left due to the British influence on these islands. Many drivers appear to enjoy the middle of the road, but these are few and far between. Driving in Trinidad is quite a thrill, a challenge to some. Cars dart in and out to pass the slower vehicles, cars that are stopped to let somebody out, or they may simply stop and chat with a passerby. However the oncoming traffic is very cordial and road rage is unheard of here. When driving the twisting-turning mountain roads, as are found on the northern sections of Trinidad and Tobago, it's a good idea to sound your horn when you approach a corner or curve so oncoming cars will know you're coming. This is important, as the roads are very narrow in many of these places.

Other vehicles are not the only hazard to roadway navigation. In the more rural areas it's not uncommon to share the road with chickens, goats, sheep, or even cows. In more urban areas, humans are known to share the road with you so drive with care.

If you don't care to rent a vehicle and try your hand at driving, you can take a taxi or rely on public transportation. All commuter transport vehicles will have a license plate that begins with the letter "H" (vehicles with the letter "H" are for hire, "P" are private vehicles, a plate that starts with a "T" is obviously a truck, and "R" plates designate a rental vehicle). Buses serve main commuter routes and are differentiated into two services, the transit and express commuter services (*ECS*). *ECS* service, (white and red-striped mini-vans), is available to points east of Port of Spain and runs along a dedicated transit highway system that only these mini-vans can use.

The most popular mode of public transport is the maxi-taxi. In Trinidad these are color-coded mini-vans. All are white and those with yellow horizontal bands run in the Port of Spain and Chaguaramas areas; red bands are for eastern Trinidad; green bands for southern Trinidad; black bands run in the Princes Town area; and brown bands run from San Fernando to the southwestern tip of the island. All vans run regular routes and the white/yellow vans that you will use in Chaguaramas have a centralized base in Port of Spain across from the port, and run every few minutes so you won't have to wait long for a ride. The usual fare is TT$2–$5, but for a few dollars more they'll usually take you a short way off their route to get you to your destination. There are larger buses that cost $2 TT and run at regular intervals, usually a couple of hours apart. These buses do not take cash, instead you must pre-purchase tickets which can be found at most marinas in Chaguaramas. A good idea is to buy a couple and keep them in your wallet or purse in case you need them. If you're headed to Chaguaramas from Port of Spain, make sure you board a taxi that says Chaguaramas on it as some don't go past Carenage.

In Scarborough you can catch a taxi headed west to the airport or Crown Point across the street from the *Ferry Terminal* and next to *KFC*. Taxis going east are located uptown, at James Square in front of the *Tobago House of Assembly*.

GOVERNMENT

Trinidad and Tobago achieved independence from Britain in 1962 followed by republican status in 1976 and is currently a member of the Commonwealth. Democratic elections are held every five years in Trinidad and Tobago (since 1956) and the voting age is 18. A Bicameral legislature exists with the President as Head of State, and executive power lying with the Prime Minister and the Cabinet. The Cabinet is made up of a Lower House (House of Representatives) and an Upper House (Senate). In Tobago, the Tobago House of Assembly is responsible for government administration on the island.

Along with the government, there is a judiciary consisting of a *Supreme Court* and several district courts. The *Supreme Court* consists of the *High Court of Justice* and the *Court of Appeals*. The *High Court of Justice* is presided over by the *Chief Justice* and 10 judges. The district courts are presided over by a chief magistrate and 7 senior and 18 stipendary magistrates.

Several nations are represented by embassies in Port of Spain. The British High Commission is located at 19 St. Clair Avenue in St. Clair and their phone number is 628-1234. The High Commission of Canada is located at Maple House, 3-3A Sweet Briar Road, St. Clair, and their phone number is 622-6232. The French Embassy is located on the 6th floor of the TATIL Building at 11 Maravel Road. Phone here is 622-7446, and their e-mail address is francett@wow.net. The German Embassy is at 7-9 Marli Street in Newtown, and their phone is 628-1630. The Vatican is represented by the Apostolic Nunciature, 11 Mary St. in St. Clair and their holy phone number is 622-5009. The Italian Consulate is at the CDC Complex on Eastern Main Road and they can be reached by phone at 662-0391. The High Commission for the Republic of India is located at 6 Victoria Ave.; their phone number is 627-7480, and their e-mail address is Hcipos@tstt.net.tt. The Venezuela Embassy is located at 16 Victoria Avenue; their phone number is 627-9821 and their e-mail address is embaveneztt@carib-link.net . The U.S. Embassy is located at 15 Queen's Park West; their phone number is 622-6371, and their e-mail address is usispos@trinidad.net.

HAM RADIO

Amateur radio operators that are citizens of signatories of the *International Amateur Radio Permit* may operate in Trinidad and Tobago without obtaining a reciprocal license. The *IARP* signatories are Argentina, Brazil, Canada, Peru, Trinidad and Tobago, USA, Uruguay and Venezuela. You may transmit normally, but you must use the "9Y4 slash" identifier before your full country call sign. U.S. hams will be able to operate in Trinidad according to their license class.

If you are a licensed amateur radio operator and are not included in the above *IARP* agreement, you can obtain a reciprocal privilege to operate in Trinidad by using the following procedures: Present an original amateur radio license with a copy. Present a passport with a copy of the identification page of the passport, and provide a description of the radio equipment to be used. The steps involved are a bit complicated, so here we go. First you must go to the Director of Telecommunications Office, 17 Abercromby Street, Third Floor, Port of Spain, Tel: 623-8060, See Mr. Bal Gunness (9Y4BG). Here a letter will be prepared which you will present to the Comptroller of Customs & Excise (Second Floor), at the corner of Abercromby Street and Independence Square, Port-of-Spain, the entrance is on Abercromby Street. Here a receipt will be prepared which you will present to the cashier at the *Ministry of Finance*, which is one floor down. The total charge involved is approximately TT$14.40. You then return the paid receipt to the second floor in the same building again to the *Comptroller of Customs & Excise*. The reciprocal license will be presented allowing operation of the amateur radio station in Trinidad and Tobago, usually for no longer than the length of time approved in your passport. Extensions are granted upon presentation of the immigration extension. To renew the license, simply show your original reciprocal license and passport to the *Comptroller of Customs and Excise*, the cost is TT$9.60. Local Trinidadian repeater frequencies are: 146.940mhz –600; 147.930mhz –600; 147.800mhz -600 (Emergency Net; Sunday net at 2000 local); 145.010mhz PACKET; and 7.159mhz with a Sunday net at 1300 zulu. For further information you can contact the Trinidad and Tobago Amateur Radio Society, Boy Scout Headquarters, St. Ann's, Trinidad, West Indies, 868-624-7271. Their e-mail address is ttars@carib-link.net.

HOLIDAYS

The only holiday period that most cruisers know of, or sometimes care about, is *Carnival* (see the section on *Carnival*). The following is a list of public holidays.

January 1–New Year's Day—New Year's Eve is known as Old Year's Night.

February-date varies—*Carnival* (see the section on *Carnival*)

February-date varies—*Eid-Ul-Fitr*. This is the beginning of the Islamic New Year. The date is determined by the position of the moon and marks the end of Ramadan and a month of fasting for Moslems.

March/April-date varies—Good Friday

March/April-date varies—Easter Sunday

March/April-date varies—Easter Monday

March/April-date varies—Spiritual Baptist Liberation Shouter Day. This holiday is in recognition of the African based religion who suffered persecution in colonial Trinidad.

May/June-date varies—Corpus Cristi

June 19—Labour Day

August 1—Emancipation Day-commemorates the abolition of slavery in 1834.

August 31—Independence Day-celebrates the emancipation from Britain in 1962.

September 24—Republic Day

October-date varies—*Diwali*. This Hindu festival celebrates Mother Lakshmi, the goddess of light and spiritual light.

December 25—Christmas Day

December 26—Boxing Day-marks the beginning of *Carnival* season.

Trinis love to party, and besides the Public Holidays, there are many other holidays, fetes, parties, and get-togethers that are celebrated regionally though they are not an official public holiday.

In February you'll find the first of four annual *Crate Races*. Originating in central Trinidad, the races have now moved to Chaguaramas where the contestants build makeshift sailing vessels, no REAL boats are allowed. A crowd favorite are the all-girl teams. *Crate Races* are also held in March, August, and October though the dates vary.

In March, the *Phagwah Festival*, based on the Indian tradition of *Holi* celebrating the arrival of Spring, is celebrated more or less nationwide and is often called the Hindu equivalent of *Carnival*. In March or April, whenever Easter falls, the Tuesday after Easter is the day of crab and goat races in Buccoo on the island of Tobago. Goat racing was introduced to Tobago from Barbados around 1925 as an alternative to horse racing. There are no saddles as the "jockeys" trots behind his swift goat that leads the way on a short length of rope. Needless to say the "jockey" needs to be a good sprinter. Nearby Pigeon Point is host to the annual *Carib International Fishing Tournament* around this same time. The third Sunday after Easter finds the town of Siparia in the southern part of Trinidad celebrating the festival of *La Divina Pastora*. The local folks, decked out in the best clothes, celebrate and make merry as the statue of the Black Madonna is marched through the streets of the town.

May is a musical month in Trinidad and Tobago. *Pan Ramajay* is a nationwide steel band festival and *Rapso* artists compete in Port of Spain for *Rapso Month*. To define *Rapso* in a few words, it's basically a musical form comprised of African, *Calypso*, and Rap musical styles.

Sometime between May and June the Islamic festival of *Hosay* is celebrated. *Hosay* is a mourning for the martyred grandsons of Mohammed, Hussein and Hassan and is best seen in the St. James suburb of Port of Spain. St. Peter's Day is usually celebrated on the last weekend of June in fishing communities all over Trinidad and Tobago. If you don't already know, St. Peter is the patron saint of fishermen.

July finds Tobago the center of celebrations with the *Charlotteville Fisherman's Fete* taking place around the middle of the month. All over Tobago, the islanders celebrate the *Tobago Heritage Festival* the last two weeks of the month. The last week in August finds Arrima celebrating the first inhabitants of Trinidad, the Amerindians, in the *Santa Rosa Festival*.

In October, Mt. Irvine, Tobago, celebrates the *Sea Festival*, a family affair with all sorts of beach activities. October showcases the *Best-Village Competition*, which is held around the middle of October. During this festival, towns all over the dual island nation sent their best craft-makers, musicians, actors, and dancers to Port of Spain for a competition. Around the end of the month is the fantastic *World Steel Band Festival*. Steel band concerts all around Trinidad show off the best of the best of *Pan* musicians. This leads up to the *Pan Jazz Festival* in November, an international event with open-air concerts featuring pan groups from around the world.

December is another month of festivity, it is the *Parang* season. *Parang* is the traditional singing of Nativity songs in clubs throughout the nation as well as door to door singing. The remarkable aspect of these songs is that they are sung in Spanish with a bit of French patois added to the mix.

HURRICANES

One of the greatest draws to the Trinidad area is the relative safety that it offers from hurricanes. Hurricane season extends from June through November with the most active period from August through the first half of October, although "off-season" storms are not at all rarities. Trinidad and Tobago are generally considered to be outside of the normal hurricane zone, and this is reflected in the wording of marine insurance policies, but if the truth be known, hurricanes, though extremely rare, are not unknown here. Between 1850 and 2000, two hurricanes and five tropical storms hit Trinidad/Tobago.

In 1933, a storm, simply called Tropical Cyclone #2, hit the southwestern tip of Trinidad with winds of over 65mph killing 13 people. The greatest storm in the modern era to hit Trinidad/Tobago was on September 30, 1963 when Hurricane *Flora* slammed into Tobago with winds in excess of 105mph. Of the 7,500 houses on the island, 2,750 were destroyed and another 3,500 damaged. Over half of the coconut and cocoa crops were destroyed and 75% of the trees in the forestry reserve fell. Tobago suffered far worse than Trinidad in that instance, damage in Trinidad was estimated at U.S. $60,000 while Tobago suffered an estimated $30 million U.S. dollars.

The last major storm to hit the islands was Tropical Storm *Alma* on August 14, 1974. With winds estimated between 40mph and 80mph, *Alma* resulted in only one death on Trinidad

In more recent years, three tropical storms hit the area in the 1990's; *Arthur* and *Fran* in 1990, and *Bret* in 1993. Like Tropical Storm *Joyce* that hit the island in 2000, none of these storms produced significant rain damage, instead there was a tremendous amount of rainfall which led to flooding and landslides.

Near misses have resulted in a significant amount of damage over the years. On August 26, 1995, Hurricane *Iris* passed some 180 miles north of Trinidad, but brought southerly winds to the area in excess of 35 mph. This created heavy seas in the Gulf of Paria and a lot of damage ashore and to vessels anchored off the western coast of Trinidad.

Hurricane *Lenny* was 400 miles away from Trinidad in the middle of the Caribbean when the his storm surge hit the islands during the period of November 18-21, 1999 causing huge seas and significant damage to the northern and western coasts of Trinidad and Tobago. On August 22, 2000, Hurricane *Debby* was passing through the northern Leewards when a feederband hit Trinidad causing severe flooding in the Barrackpore area.

While you have a better than average chance of not seeing a tropical storm or hurricane during your visit to Trinidad/Tobago, don't get complacent. If a major storm threatens, I would suggest Laguna Grande in the Golfo de Carriacou, Venezuela, but give yourself at least 48 hours to get there.

INTERNET IN TRINIDAD AND TOBAGO

Internet access is easy in Trinidad, and not too difficult in Tobago either. In the *Services Appendix* in the back of this guide you'll find a listing of Internet access sites in Trinidad and Tobago along with their phone numbers and e-mail addresses.

In Chaguaramas most of the Internet access businesses also have a limited display of stationery and office supplies, as well as fax and phone service. *Crews Inn* has the *Mariner's Office* on A-dock under the *Lighthouse Restaurant*, you can also ship and receive packages here. *Coral Cove Marina* houses *Cyber Sea*, IMS is home to *Island Surf Cafe*, and *Ocean Internet* has access sites at *Peake's, Power Boats,* and *Tardieu*.

If you're at *TTSA* you can stroll down to the *Chaguaramas Hotel and Convention Center* to *SameSame* for Internet service. In Port of Spain you can access the net at *Netsurf* at *Starlite Plaza*.

In Scarborough, Tobago, the public library sits across the street from the ferry docks and offers free Internet access. In Charlotteville the public library there is equally as accommodating. Also in town is the *Charlotteville Beach Bar and Restaurant* who have just come online. In Crown Point there are several places to surf the net. The *Tourism Office* at the airport offers online service as does the *Cyber Cafe*, also at the airport. Just down the road from the airport is the *Clothes Wash Cafe* where you can wash your clothes as you surf. A bit further on is the *Original Pancake House*, now online as well.

There are hundreds of websites relating to Trinidad and Tobago. Some of the best sites of interest are listed below.

www.boatersenterprise.com
The website of The Boca.

www.callaloo.co.tt
Trini artist Peter Minshall's *Callaloo Carnival Company* site. Minshall is an artist who works in the medium of *mas*, a tradition of performance and celebration indigenous to *Carnival*.

www.caribwx.com
David Jones' *Caribbean Weather Center Ltd.*

www.hartsCarnival.com
Harts Carnival camp page with the latest *Carnival* news.

www.tidco.tt
This is another TIDCO site with trade and tourism information.

www.trinibase.com
Lots of stats and Carnival links.

www.trinidadexpress.com
For the latest news.

LEAVING YOUR BOAT IN TRINIDAD

Many skippers have insurance policies with "named windstorm" clauses necessitating the vessel be out of the maximum risk zone for hurricanes by a certain date, usually July 1st. Some clauses use the latitude of 12° 30.00' N, while others use 12° 30.00' N, which is approximately in the middle of Prickly Bay, Grenada. Either way, Trinidad is well south of this latitude and is a favorite spot for yachtsmen to leave their boat during hurricane season.

Chaguaramas, as you will learn, has several large yards with hundreds of boats on the hard for long periods of time. You too can take advantage of this hurricane-free paradise, but there are certain steps that must be taken.

First, your boat must be left in the care of a yard

or marina, and a letter prepared by the marina or yard, called a *Temporary Importation of Foreign Yachts Form,* along with an inventory of items aboard, must be taken to the *Customs* office for approval. The captain and crew must also submit letters for *Immigration* approval, this is extremely important if the crew remains while the captain leaves the country. The ships storage papers will need to be presented upon the captain's or owner's return.

The costs involved are generally the same at all the yards, with *Crews Inn* being perhaps a little higher than the rest, but then again, they primarily cater to the larger vessels. *Peakes, IMS,* and *Crews Inn* all advertise multi-hull rates. Bear in mind that I cannot quote rates here as they are not cast in stone and may change by the time this guide is published, especially with the TT gaining against the U.S. dollar.

Long-term storage rates are also fairly uniform with multi-hull rates generally running about twice the rate of a monohull.

MEDICAL EMERGENCIES

Trinidad and Tobago are well covered by medical facilities so assistance is not too far away. For a complete listing of hospitals and their phone numbers see *Appendix D.*

There is no malaria in Trinidad and Tobago, and only rare occurrences of Dengue fever, which the government normally takes immediate action to contain. If you plan to head to Trinidad, and even further south to Venezuela (especially if you're heading inland), Guiana, or Brazil, you should check with the *Communicable Disease Center's (CDC)* website for the latest in health warnings and take appropriate precautions.

PHONING HOME

The phone system in Trinidad and Tobago is very good and quite easy to use. Most public phones use a card though some still take coins. *TSTT (Telecommunication Service of Trinidad and Tobago)* phone cards are sold in most stores and marinas. The area code for Trinidad and Tobago is 868 and the emergency number in both islands is 999.

PROPANE

If you are in Chaguaramas and need propane you have two choices, and the easiest way is to make use of *Ian's Taxi.* Ian, who monitors VHF ch. 68, makes his propane runs on Tuesdays and requests that you leave your empty propane bottles at the dockmaster's office at any of the major marinas by 0800. Making sure you leave the proper amount of money in an envelope for him and that your boat's name is stenciled on your tank. Ian charges TT$1.05 per pound plus a TT$25 fee per tank. This amounts to TT$46 for a 20lb tank and TT$35.50 for a 10lb tank. Have your tank in to at the offices of *Power Boats, Crews Inn,* or *TTSA,* or *TTYC* by 0800 and Ian will have your tank back to you that afternoon. Call Ian on VHF ch. 68 for more info on current rates, time and places of pickups. If you have a car, you might wish to drive out to the *Ramco* filling station south of Port of Spain. From Chaguaramas head into Port of Spain on the *Western Main Road* passing the stadium and heading south past the port. Continue past the *Uriah Butler Highway,* past the *Johnson & Johnson* building, take your next left, and *Ramco* will be on your right

In Tobago, check with *Viking Dive Shop* at the *Pigeon Point Resort* for help with acquiring propane.

PROVISIONING AND SHOPPING

Trinidad is a great place to provision, especially if you are heading back up-island or to Venezuela. Although some things in Venezuela will be cheaper, your selection of items in Trinidad, at least for Americans and Canadians, will be brands that you will recognize and with which you are familiar. In Venezuela you'll find a lot of brands that you've never seen before and a lot of items manufactured in Venezuela with Spanish labels, so brush up on s*u Espanol* before shopping in Margarita.

In Chaguaramas, you'll find good shopping at *Hi-Lo* at *Crews Inn Marina* and at the store in *Power Boats.* Jesse James' *Members Only Maxi-Taxi Service* offers several good shopping trips for those interested in bulk purchasing. Every couple of weeks or so, Jesse will arrange for a trip to *Price Smart* in Chaguanas (TT$45 for the round trip). *Price Smart* is a membership store similar to *Sam's Club* and you can shop there on Jesse's card. There is a new *Price Smart* being built across from the stadium in downtown Port of Spain.

On Friday's Jesse normally runs to the *Tru Valu* store at *Long Circular Mall*, a popular grocery shopping expedition that is free (cruisers also get a 3% discount on their purchases). On the road that parallels the covered parking lot there is a small open-air market where you can pick up fresh produce.

Occasionally Jesse makes runs to the *Grand Bazaar Mall* for shopping at the *X-tra* store, another good grocery store. On Saturdays, very early, Jesse makes a run to the fresh veggie and fish market in Port of Spain, this is a must for a good deal on fruits, vegetables, fish, and meat. Jesse also makes occasional trips to the *Food Giant* in Barataria. For more information call Jesse or his wife Sharon, *Member's Only* on VHF ch. 68. I know a lot of you may think that I'm making a big deal by pushing Jesse's service. Let me explain. I take no ads. I receive no perks. I receive no freebies. Nor do I seek them. Jessie has given me nothing for mentioning his service. To the best of my ability I relate to you, the cruiser in need of information, what is available, and Jesse does the cruising community a great service, and is the only person that does this.

A short walk west of *TTYC* is a small strip mall with a *Hi-Lo* grocery, *Glencoe Pharmacy*, a hardware store, bank, and several restaurants (French, Chinese, and BBQ). *Westmoorings Mall*, a mile or two east of *TTYC* is another popular stop. Here too is a *Hi-Lo* (open on Sunday's till noon), as well as *Nelson's 1-Hour Photo*, a great food court, and dozens of good stores. The *ATM* outside the bank will give you cash in TT or US$. By the time this guide is published, *Hi-Lo* will have moved into its new home next to the mall. As a final note, there is a *Super K-Mart* being built in Port of Spain. Port of Spain also has two *Radio Shack* outlets, one at *Consumer Electronics*, the other at *Electronic Components*. These are great places to pick up an alarm system with a motion detector before heading to Venezuela. Why do you need a motion detector in Venezuela? Read on . . .

SECURITY

One of the greatest concerns of cruisers in the Caribbean is crime. I would love to paint a picture of a tropical Eden, but that would be a lie. Crime does exist here, crimes upon cruisers does exist, but it is a fact of life that we deal with here and simple precautions will usually keep you out of harm's way.

First and foremost, avoid high-risk anchorages, and buddy-boat for safety's sake, currently this is a special concern for vessels transiting the waters off the northern shore of Venezuela between Trinidad and Margarita. You'll learn of these trouble spots by talking to other cruisers or by listening to the *Safety and Security Net*, which we will learn about in a moment. When leaving your vessel, lock it, hatches and large ports, don't leave an opening for a skinny child to enter (don't laugh!) and don't leave items on deck that you do not want stolen. At night, you might also wish to lock yourself inside your boat so you don't wake up with an intruder hovering above you. The choice of carrying weapons aboard is strictly a personal one, I prefer to have one and not need it that need one and not have it, but that's just me. Some folks like to keep a flare gun handy as well as a spotlight for blinding intruders in the night. Don't laugh at a flare gun, it can be a very effective weapon.

One of the greatest temptations for a thief is your dinghy, *lock it or lose it* as is the motto of the *Safety and Security Net*. You can usually tell someone who has cruised in the Caribbean, they often have their dinghy hoisted in the air at night. Some of us don't do that, preferring instead to use a wire cable and lock, but either way, a good thief can still get away with your dinghy despite your best efforts.

A lot of cruisers try to make their dinghy look as unappealing as possible by joining in a competition to see who can have the ugliest outboard motor. Thieves tend to concentrate on those nice, new looking outboards, ones that look like they have a long life ahead of them. Here again, *lock it or lose it*. Don't keep anything in your dinghy that you don't want stolen, not that these items will be stolen, just don't take that chance. Another idea is not painting the name of your boat on it such as "Tender To My Boat." This only informs people when you are NOT on your boat. If you plan to travel about on land in questionable areas, and you will learn where they are by talking to other cruisers or listening to the *Safety and Security Net*, do not advertise by wearing a lot of jewelry. Keep your money safe in your pocket or other location. Women, this means that you should keep your cash on your person instead of in a purse or fanny pack as people have been known to sneak up from behind and slice the strap on a purse or fanny pack and make off with it. If you're attending *Carnival*, keep your money in your shoe as there are pickpockets working the crowd with surgical precision. If you're walking about at night, do so in a group, there is strength in numbers.

Practice security and soon it will become second nature. If you need the help of the Police in Trinidad and Tobago, the emergency number is 999.

Vessels equipped with SSB receivers can tune in to the *Caribbean Safety and Security Net* on 8104 at 0815 daily. Currently maintained by Melodye and John Pompa on the S/V *Second Millenium*, the *Safety and Security Net*, sometimes jokingly referred to as the *Moan and Complain Net* by its detractors, offers cruisers the latest scoop on what's going on where. If a dinghy has been stolen in St. Vincent, you'll likely hear about it here. If the Montserrat volcano is acting up, you might here about it here also. If somebody was robbed while walking down the streets of some Caribbean town at night, you'll learn about that also. What's to gain? Well, you'll learn where to take special security measures and what areas you might wish to avoid. Besides accessing the net on SSB, you can e-mail the net at boatmillie@aol.com.

TIDES AND CURRENTS

Vessels heading to Trinidad or Tobago from points north, particularly from Grenada or Carriacou, will encounter strong and fluky currents in the stretch of water between Grenada and Trinidad and Tobago. The *Equatorial Current* (*Guyana Current*) flows northwestward between Trinidad/Tobago and Grenada and to say it is unpredictable would be an understatement. Heading for a waypoint at Boca del Monos from Grenada, you will find that the current is pushing you westward at over 2 knots at times, while just a few minutes later the current will appear to be non-existent. The strength of this current is lessened somewhat on an ebbing tide which flows southeast.

This current makes sailing from Grenada to Tobago difficult at best. A better suggestion would be to head for Tobago from Petite St. Vincent, or even Barbados. Entering the harbor at Scarborough on Tobago, you might encounter an eastward flowing current, an eddy that has spun off the westward setting *Equatorial Current*.

The current flows northwestward between Tobago and Trinidad and then westward closer in along the northern coast of Trinidad and sometimes attains a velocity of 2–3 knots. At places along the northern coast you can sometimes pick up a bit of an easterly flow when the tide ebbs and flows southeast between Tobago and Trinidad.

Approaching the northwestern tip of Trinidad at the Bocas del Dragon, you will want to exercise caution when entering Boca del Monos, the normal passage for yachts heading into Chaguaramas Bay (try to time your arrival for daylight hours here). When the prevailing winds and seas are up, and the tidal flow is heading north through the bocas, you can have some heavy sea action well into the boca as the current sometimes flows northward through here at up to 4 knots on the flood. On the other hand, no matter the tide, the current rarely if ever has a noticeable southerly flow through the Bocas. The current that flows through the Bocas, and for a distance along the northern coast as far as Macqueripe, is known locally as *les remous*.

The current along the western shore of Trinidad, as well as the tides, are impacted by the weather conditions in Venezuela. Heavy rains and flooding in the Orinoco delta region releases tremendous amounts of water and energy into the Gulf of Paria. This force has nowhere to go except towards Trinidad and can make itself apparent in the form of higher tides, stronger swirling currents, and lot of flotsam and jetsam approaching from the Gulf. The entire western coast of Trinidad, from the Bocas to Icacos, is washed by a southerly-southeasterly eddy of this northward flowing current

Chaguaramas has its own particular problems with currents as well. Sometimes, anchored boats will spin and turn and bounce off each other, so use caution when anchored in Chaguaramas Bay. In *TTYC*, you'll often rock slightly when the tide changes and the wind dies, but this won't last long.

Entering Port of Spain, the current flows at a velocity of about ½ knot southeast on the flood and 1½ knots on the ebb. This is due to an eddy action of the main flow of current, which runs generally northeast through the Bocas.

The current along the southern shore of Trinidad is extremely strong, usually 3-5 knots, and I've been told by local mariners that they've seen it flow as strong as 7 knots.

The tidal range in Trinidad and Tobago is approximately 3'. Tide tables can be found in the *Trinidad and Tobago Boaters Directory* available free at most marinas, chandleries, at the *Boca* offices, and at *YSATT*.

TIME

Trinidad and Tobago are on *Atlantic Standard Time* (*AST*), one hour earlier than *Eastern Standard Time*. If it is noon in Atlanta, it's 1100 in Chaguaramas, however there is no daylight saving time in Trinidad and Tobago so, from April through November, the islands will be on the same time as the eastern U.S. Atlantic seaboard.

VHF

Usage of the VHF radio in Trinidad/Tobago is similar to usage rules in most other places in the Caribbean. Channel 16 is used as a hailing and distress frequency and ch. 70 is for digital use only. Most cruisers in TT tend to use 68 has a hailing channel though it is also often used by local commercial vessels and the TT *Coast Guard*.

In Chaguaramas there is a daily net beginning at 0800 on channel 68 and lasting for about 20 minutes or so. This is an informative net for newcomers, and a place to ask for assistance in finding parts and services. During the *Treasures of the Bilge* segment, you will be allowed to advertise those items you don't need and wish to trade or barter (it is illegal for cruisers to sell anything in Trinidad/Tobago, but foreign flag vessels may trade or barter between themselves).

Is is requested that cruisers not use the following VHF channels while in Chaguaramas for boat to boat communications as they are in use by the following businesses or agencies:

01 *Echo Marine*
8–17 *Coast Guard*
11 *Tidewater Tugs*
69 *Peakes*
70 digital only
72 *Power Boats*
74 *Caribbean Dry Dock*
77 *Crews Inn*
25–28, 78 *North Post Radio*
84–88 Public Correspondence/Marine Operator

The recommended general usage channels are: 1, 5, 7A, 18A, 19A, 21A, 22A, 23A, 61, 62, 63, 65A, 66A, 71, 78A, 79A, 80A, 82A, 83A, 85A, 88A.

As you approach Trinidad from Grenada listen for *North Post Radio*'s strong signal on VHF ch. 16 for notices to mariners.

WEATHER

The outstanding feature for mariners in the islands of Trinidad and Tobago is the steadiness of the easterly trade winds. The Tradewinds blow about 80% of the time year round. Winds from the east and southeast are particularly dominant in summer when the Bermuda High has shifted north while northeasterlies are more prominent from around November through April and give way to easterly and southeasterly winds in the spring. During the summer months the easterly wave occurs and is characterized by winds out of the east/northeast ahead of the wave and followed by an east/southeast wind. In summer the trades tend to lessen at night and strengthen during the day. Gale-force winds are rare, but they can occur within a severe thunderstorm, or as an effect of a passing tropical storm or hurricane.

Weather coverage is usually quite good in the islands of Trinidad and Tobago, especially if you have an SSB or HF receiving capabilities. Perhaps the most popular weather report is given by Eric Mackie, 9Z4CP, on the *Caribbean Emergency and Weather Net* that meets daily at 0630 on 7.162 MHz, lower sideband, and at 1830 on 3,815 MHz, also lower sideband. The net begins with check-ins until five minutes into the schedule when official weather reports are given. Then Eric, a TV weatherman in Trinidad, comes on with his own weather observations. Mobile Maritime ham operators are welcome to give their weather observations while underway as Eric uses these reports to assist him in creating and verifying his forecasts. If you can't find the net in the morning on 7.162, try them on 3.815 MHz, lower sideband.

Another popular weather forecaster is David Jones who operates from his base in Tortola, BVI. David is on the air each day at 0830 AST (1215-1230 UTC) on 8.104 MHz. He begins with a 24-48 hour wind and sea summary followed by a synoptic analysis and tropical conditions during hurricane season. After this, David repeats the weather for those needing fills and finally he takes check-ins reporting local conditions from sponsoring vessels (vessels who have paid an annual fee for David's service). David moves up to 12.359 at 0900 AST or whenever he is finished with his normal broadcast on 8104, whichever is later. This frequency often works better for those vessels in Trinidad, Tobago, and Venezuela. During hurricane season David relays the latest tropical storm advisories at 1815 AST on 6.224 MHz.

It is also possible to pick up the guru of weather forecasters, Herb Hilgenberg, *Southbound II*, from Canada. Herb operates from his home in Canada and you can tune in to Herb on 12.359 MHz, upper sideband, at 2000 Zulu.

Another weather option is *Alex's Net*. Transmitting from Margarita, Alex can be picked up on 4054 MHz, upper sideband, daily at 0700, and on 8155 MHz, upper sideband, daily at 0730.

Another well-respected forecaster is a ham operator named George, KP2G. George can be found on the *Caribbean Maritime Mobile Net* located at 7.241 MHz, lower sideband at 0715 AST, 15 minutes into the net. George gives an overview of the current Caribbean weather beginning in Trinidad and working his way up the chain to Puerto Rico. At 0730 AST, George moves to 7.086, lower sideband for further Caribbean weather information and questions and answers. Then another ham transmits the same weather information in a weatherfax format.

On 4.426, 6.501, 8.764, 13.089, and 17.314 MHz, you can pick up the voice weather broadcasts from NMN four times a day at 0500, 1100, 1700, and 2300 EST.

North Post Radio gives weather reports at 0940 and 1640 daily on VHF ch. 27.

Trinidad and Tobago have a wealth of AM and FM stations where you can receive weather periodically during the day. On the AM band you can tune in to *NBS Radio* at 0610, and *Radio Trinidad* at 730 on your dial.

On the FM band, the popular *Hott 93* (93.5) has a local forecast every morning at 0730. Other FM stations with periodic weather broadcasts are *Central Radio* (90.5), *Radio ICN* (91.1), *Love* (94.1), *The Rock* (95.1), *WEFM* (96), *Music Radio 97* (97.1), *YesFM* (98.9), *NBS Radio* (100), *Power 102* (102.5), *WABC* (103), *Radio 104* (104), *Radio Tempo* (105), *Classic Radio* (106).

YSATT

While Trinidad is known far and wide in the cruising community for it's plethora of marine services and the quality of the work performed, the marine industry is actually very young on the island. In 1994, a gentleman named Donald Stollmeyer, who also opened *Power Boats* in the early 1990's, founded YSATT, the *Yacht Service Association of Trinidad and Tobago*. YSATT, pronounced "y-sat", is a non-profit organization established by the boatyards and marinas in the Chaguaramas peninsula to ensure the proper and controlled growth of the marine service industry in Trinidad and Tobago.

The yachting industry in Trinidad is relatively young, only about 10 years old, but it has grown considerably in that decade to include several good yards and a growing labor force. *YSATT* is intent on maintaining and improving the quality of services provided to visiting boaters in Trinidad by screening, training, and monitoring its members, as well as advising government agencies of the *YSATT* position on relative legal issues. The organization also keeps a database of correspondence received from cruisers about their experiences, good and bad, while in Trinidad.

The *YSATT* office is located at *Crews Inn*, almost next door to *Trump Tours*. Here you'll find Dianne who'll be glad to help you review any and all correspondence about a particular service you are inquiring about in Trinidad and find positive referrals to fill your needs.

YSATT also has a formal process to deal with complaints against and by boatyards and cruisers. People with a serious complaint, whether it's a cruiser that received a slipshod repair, or a member that has not received payment, will go to work to sort out the problem. But don't just run to *YSATT* with your problem. You must first bring the complaint to the attention of the member and give them the opportunity to rectify the matter. Only if this fails should you submit a written complaint to *YSATT*. For more details on the complaint process, visit Diane in the *YSATT* office.

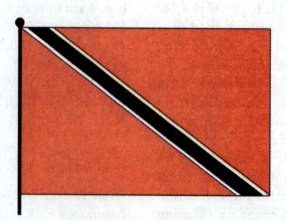

Flag of Trinidad/Tobago

Using the Charts

To gather the soundings used in this guide I use a computer-based hydrographic system in my data acquisition vessel, a 12' Carib RIB (*Afterglow*, the tender to *IV Play*) graciously supplied by *Inflatable Xperts* in Ft. Lauderdale, Fla. The system consists of an off-the-shelf GPS and sonar combination that gives a GPS waypoint and depth every two seconds including the time of each observation. The software used records and stores this information in an onboard computer. When I begin to chart an area, I first put *Afterglow's* bow on a well-marked, prominent point of land and take GPS lat/lons for a period of at least five minutes (I used to do this for twenty minutes before the rolling back of SA). I use the average of all these positions to check against the lat/lon shown on the topos that I use to create the charts. I also use cross bearings to help set up control points for my own reference. At this point I then begin to take soundings.

My next objective is to chart the inshore reefs. Then I'll plot all visible hazards to navigation. These positions are recorded by hand on my field notes as well as being recorded electronically. I rely primarily on my on-site notes for the actual construction of the charts. The soundings taken by the system are later entered by hand but it is the field notes that help me create the basis for the chart graphics. The computer will not tell me where a certain reef ends or begins as accurately as I can record it and show it on my field notes. Next I will run the one-fathom line as well as the ten-fathom line (if applicable) and chart these. Here is where the system does most of the work though I still stop to take field notes. Finally, I will crisscross the entire area in a grid pattern and hopefully catch hazards that are at first glance unseen. It is not unusual to spend days sounding an area of only a couple of square miles. This takes a lot of fuel as well as a lot of time when transferring the data to the chart!

Due to the speed of *Afterglow*, each identical lat/long may have as many as 5-10 separate soundings. Then, with the help of NOAA tide tables, the computer gives me accurate depths to one decimal place for each separate lat/long pair (to two decimal places) acquired on the data run. A macro purges all but the lowest depths for each lat/long position (to two decimal places). At this point the actual plotting is begun including one fathom and ten fathom lines. The charts themselves are still constructed from outline tracings of topographic maps and the lat/long lines are placed in accordance with these maps.

These charts are as accurate as I can make them and I believe them to be superior to any others. They are indeed more detailed than all others showing many areas that are not covered, or are incorrectly represented by other publications. However, it is not possible to plot every individual rock or coral head so pilotage by eye is still essential. On many of the routes in my guides you must be able to pick out the blue, deeper water as it snakes between sandbanks, rocky bars, and coral heads. Learn to trust your eyes. Remember that on the banks, sandbars and channels can shift over time so that once what was a channel may now be a sandbar. Never approach a cut or sandbar with the sun in your eyes, it should be above and behind you. Sunglasses with a polarized lens can be a big help in combating the glare of the sun on the water. With good visibility the sandbars and heads stand out and are clearly defined. As you gain experience you may even learn to read the subtle differences in the water surface as it flows over underwater obstructions.

All courses shown are magnetic. All GPS latitude and longitude positions for entrances to cuts and for detouring around shoal areas are only to be used in a general sense. They are meant to get you into the general area, you must pilot your way through the cut or around the shoal yourself. You will have to keep a good lookout, GPS will not do that for you. The best aids to navigation when near these shoals and cuts are sharp eyesight and good light. The charts will show both deep draft vessel routes as well as some shallow draft vessel routes. Deep draft vessel routes will accommodate a draft of 6' minimum and often more with the assistance of the tide. Shallow draft vessel routes are for dinghies and small outboard powered boats with drafts of less than 3'. Shallow draft monohulls and multihulls very often use these same routes.

Not being a perfect world, I expect errors to occur. I would deeply appreciate any input and corrections that you may notice as you travel these waters. Please send your suggestions to Stephen J. Pavlidis, C/O Seaworthy Publications, Inc., 215 S. Park St., Port Washington, WI. 53074-5553. If you see me anchored nearby, don't hesitate to stop and say hello and offer your input. Your suggestion may help improve the next edition of this guide.

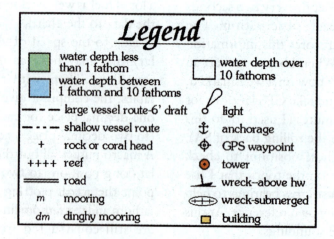

CAUTION: *The Index charts are designed strictly for orientation, they are NOT to be used for navigational purposes. All charts are to be used in conjunction with the text. All soundings are in feet at Mean Low Water. All courses are magnetic. Projection is Transverse Mercator. Datum is WGS84. North is always "up" on these charts.*

List of Charts

The prudent navigator will not rely solely on any single aid to navigation, particularly on floating aids.

Differences in latitude and longitude may exist between these charts and other charts of the area; therefore the transfer of positions from one chart to another should be done by bearings and distances from common features.

The author and publisher take no responsibility for errors, omissions, or the misuse of these charts. No warranties are either expressed or implied as to the usability of the information contained herein. Always keep a good lookout when piloting in these waters.

■ TRINIDAD

TRI-1	Trinidad and Approaches	35
TRI-2	Bocas del Dragon	36
TRI-3	Monos Island, Morris Bay Grand Fond Bay	36
TRI-4	Scotland Bay	37
TRI-5	Chacachacare	39
TRI-6	Chaguaramas Bay	42
TRI-7	Gaspar Grande Island, Bombshell Bay to Bayview Marina	46
TRI-8	Gaspar Grand Island, Wynn's Bay (Corsair Bay)	47
TRI-9	Chaguaramas Bay to Port of Spain	48
TRI-10	Carenage Anchorage, TTSA	49
TRI-11	Cumana Bay, TTYC	52
TRI-12	Port of Spain	53
TRI-13	Point-a-Pierre	58
TRI-14	Saut d'Eau Island to La Vache Point	61
TRI-15	La Vache Point to Point Parasol	63
TRI-16	Point Parasol to Chupara	67

■ TOBAGO

TOB-1	Tobago and Approaches	72
TOB-2	Rockly Bay, Scarborough	73
TOB-3	Crown Point to Pigeon Point	76
TOB-4	Buccoo Reef	78
TOB-5	Mt. Irvine Bay to Grafton Bay	81
TOB-6	Great Courland Bay, Plymouth	82
TOB-7	Castara Bay	86
TOB-8	Englishman's Bay	88
TOB-9	Parlatuvier Bay	89
TOB-10	Man of War Bay, Charlotteville	90
TOB-11	Northeastern Tip, The Melville Islands, St. Giles Island, London Bridge	93
TOB-12	Tyrrel's Bay, Speyside	94
TOB-13	King's Bay	96

Index Charts

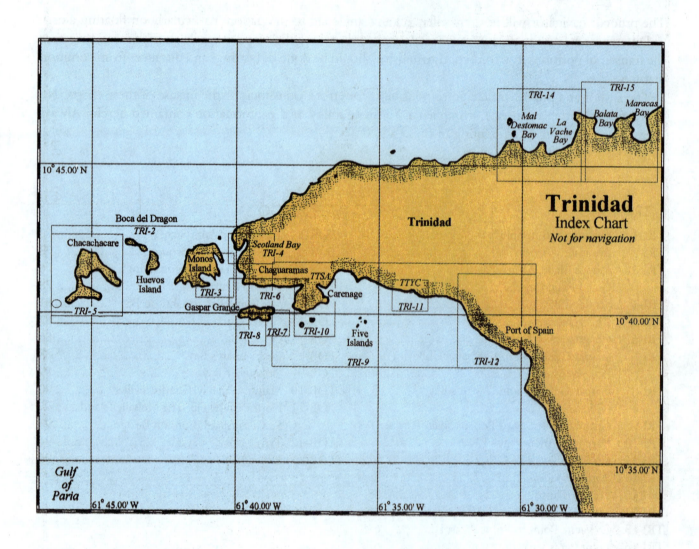

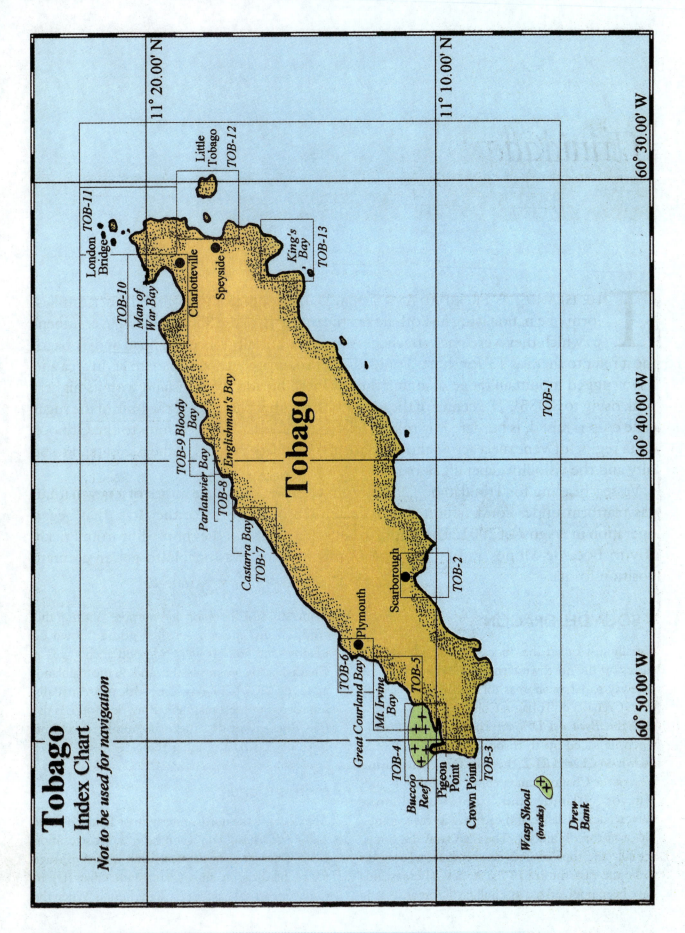

Trinidad

THE ISLANDS OF TRINIDAD AND TOBAGO, the southernmost of the Lesser Antilles, form one nation lying just off the northeastern tip of the South American continent to which they were once attached. Although officially called Trinidad and Tobago, most refer to them as TT for short. Trinidad is approximately 1864 square miles in area and has a rugged mountain range spanning the northern breadth of the island with its highest peak rising to 3,085'. The center of the island, a flat central plain where the bulk of the sugar cane crop is raised, is bordered by rolling hills to the south. The proximity to the Orinoco delta region of Venezuela across the Gulf of Paria is why the waters of the island tend to be silty and the visibility generally poor.

Vessels heading for Trinidad or Tobago from Grenada should be aware of a new natural gas platform under construction approximately 25 miles north of the Boca that began operation in August of 2001. The platform lies just a bit east of the rhumb line from Prickly Bay to Boca de Monos and by the time of this writing I was unable to get an accurate position for it.

BOCA DEL DRAGON

Usually just called the "bocas," these islands and passes off the northwestern tip of Trinidad are the gateway to Chaguaramas for vessels approaching from Grenada or Tobago. Columbus named these cuts the *Boca del Dragon*, the *Dragon's Mouth*, when he sailed north through them in 1498. As shown on Chart TRI-2, there are three islands lying west of the Chaguaramas peninsula, Monos Island, Huevos Island, and the westernmost, Chacachacare Island, and each has its own unique bit of history behind it. The islands of the bocas, actually the tops of undersea mountains, are said to be the easternmost of the Andes. These islands have been popularized as a holiday resort and many Trinis still visit them for that purpose. Visiting this compact archipelago is called going "down de islands" and cruisers will find good anchorages at Chacachacare, Monos Island, and on the mainland, at lovely Scotland Bay. The Bocas are usually numbered by local mariners. Boca de Monos is the first Boca, Boca de Huevos is number two, and Boca de Navios is number three.

Monos Island

Approaching the northwestern tip of Trinidad at the *Bocas del Dragon*, you will need to exercise caution when entering *Boca de Monos*, the normal passage for yachts heading into Chaguaramas Bay (try to time your arrival here for daylight hours). When the

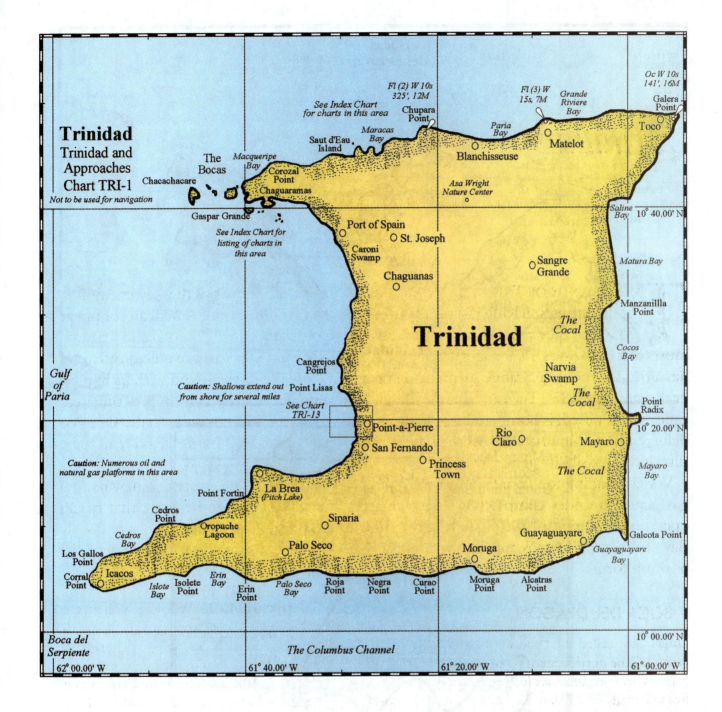

prevailing winds and seas are up, and the tidal flow is heading north through the bocas, you can have some heavy sea action well into the boca as the current sometimes flows northward through here at up to 4 knots on the flood (as a side note, there is no south setting current on the ebb in *Boca de Monos*).

As shown on Chart TRI-2, a GPS waypoint at 10° 43.00' N, 61° 40.50' W, will place you approximately ½ mile north of the entrance to *Boca de Monos*. As I mentioned, try to arrive here in daylight and use caution if the sea conditions are creating rough seas in the boca. The passage is wide and quite deep as you pass between the mainland of Trinidad to port, and Le Chapeau, the small rock that lies northeast of Monos Island. If entering at night, Le Chapeau is has a light that flashes white (3) every 10 seconds. Soon, as the effects of the seas north of the bocas fade away, the waters in the *Boca de Monos* will become calmer. To port the

TRINIDAD • 35

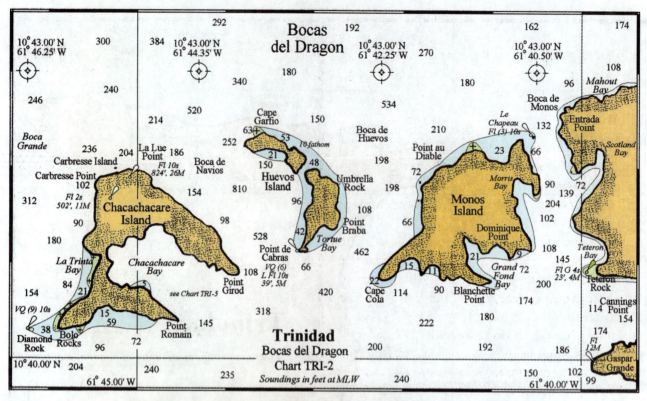
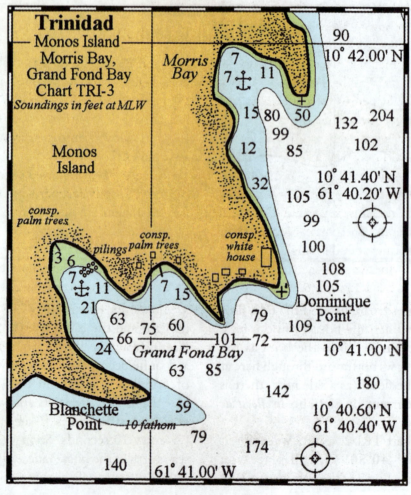

entrance to Scotland Bay will open up just past the small off-lying rock on your port side (for more information on Scotland Bay see the next section). Continuing on past Teteron Rock (Fl G, 4s, 23', 4M) you can make your turn to port to enter Chaguaramas Bay. On the eastern shore of Monos Islands are two anchorages, Morris Bay and Grand Fond Bay. Although open to the southeast, both anchorages are remarkably calm in light to moderate southeast winds.

The anchorage at Morris Bay lies just west of Blanchette Point as shown on Chart TRI-3. Upon entering give the shallow bar south of Blanchette Point a wide berth and head towards the northwestern corner of the bay for the best holding. The houses onshore are private and visits should be by invitation only.

The anchorage at Great Fond Bay lies west of Dominique Point as shown on Chart TRI-3. Head towards the northwestern corner of the bay to anchor in 15'–25' of water. You'll notice some old pilings here that date to World War II when the owners of this island called the cove *Allies Bay* to distance themselves from any association with the Axis powers. Grand Fond Bay is sometimes called Turtle Bay due to the leatherback turtles that nest here.

Monos was originally named by the Spanish and it means *apes*, probably due to the howler monkeys that share the island with a few Trinis who have private homes here. There was once a thriving whaling station on Monos and I'm told that if one searches in the shallows off the point at Grand Fond Bay you can see the remains of the old cauldrons that were used to render the whale blubber. I've looked for them and cannot find them, but perhaps I've been looking in the wrong place. If anybody knows where they are I'd appreciate a pointer.

Today, part of the island is owned by the well-known Gatcliffe family. Tommy Gatcliffe is said to be one of two people who knows the secret formula for the world-famous Angostura Bitters.

At the southeastern end of Boca de Monos you'll find Teteron Bay, the home of the *Trinidad and Tobago Naval Station*. The bay is restricted and anchoring is not permitted. The house on the point was turned into a bar called the *Crow's Nest* by the U.S. military during WW II.

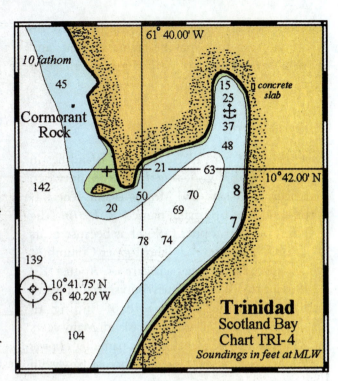

Scotland Bay

Scotland Bay is one of the loveliest anchorages in Trinidadian waters and is my personal favorite. As shown on Chart TRI-2 and TRI-4, Scotland Bay lies on the mainland side of *Boca de Monos* and works its way deep into the surrounding mountains. As you enter the bay you'll likely see boats anchored off the beaches on your port, or off the mainland to your starboard, but the best anchorage is tucked up in the northern tip of the bay in 20'–40' of water. Drop your hook between the small beach on your left and the concrete slab to your right where people sometimes camp. The bottom here is mud and the holding is good. You'll find that you'll rarely be alone here, especially on the weekends when local boaters come here to get away from it all for a while. A good idea is to anchor bow to the south and set a stern anchor to the north or tie a stern line to a tree on shore.

Scotland Bay is wonderful for observing wildlife. Here you'll hear the lion-like roar of the howler monkeys, especially after a good rain. At night, you will need to put up screens and set a light in your cockpit to help keep away the fruit bats. They've been known to enter boats at night, feast on whatever fresh fruit may be laying around, and leave a layer of nasty, slick, guano all over everything.

Huevos Island

As shown on Chart TRI-2, Huevos Island lies in the middle of the *Boca del Dragon* between Chacachacare Island and Monos Island. The 84-acre island was originally named *El Delfin* (the dolphin) by Christopher Columbus because of its appearance. It is said that Christopher Columbus, while anchored off Chacachacare on August 12, 1498, sent two skiffs to Huevos in search of water and the returning sailors told of finding an abandoned fishing village on the island. Many years later, Spanish settlers changed its name to *Huevos* (eggs) because of the large number of hawksbill turtle eggs laid on the island's beach.

In 1900 Huevos Island was owned by Johnny Wehekind, a keen fisherman who loved the piscatorial action in the surrounding waters. In 1927, Huevos Island was sold to Carl Boos for $1 including the M/V *El Pao*, by the headman of Seville in Venezuela. The Boos family's hospitality was known far and wide and they hosted Royalty and world leaders such as the Duke and Duchess of Kent in 1935, Princes Margaret in 1958, and Franklin Delano Roosevelt who came here to fish during WWII. Today the island is still owned by the Boos family.

Huevos is actually two islands, and the break between the two is called *Boca Sin Entrada* (*Mouth with no entry*). There is a group of submerged rocks abreast of the break that is said to be haunted. It is said that on calm moonlit nights you can hear the sound of a chapel bell and the solemn chanting of ancient Latin hymns. Legend has it that a Spanish galleon was wrecked here and during the last moments, a prince, a passenger aboard the vessel, and his chaplain summoned a group of choirboys that were aboard to beg God for deliverance from the danger.

If you remember reading about oilbirds, you might be interested to know that one of their eight known colonies on Trinidad is on Huevos Island.

Chacachacare Island

Usually just referred to as Chacachacare, this 900-acre island is the westernmost of the *Boca del Dragon* chain and the last bit of Trinidad before you reach the coastline of Venezuela some 7 miles to the west.

Mountainous and wooded, Chacachacare is named after the native cotton that grows on the island, *chaca* (sometimes written as *chac-chac*) in Amerindian. Artifacts have placed the earliest settlers on Chacachacare between 100–700 A.D. The first European to sight Chacachacare was Christopher Columbus who anchored here on August 12, 1498. He named the bay he anchored in *Puerto de Gato* for the wild cats that he heard on shore. Those wild cats were actually the howler monkeys and they DO sound like wild cats. Columbus named the island *El Caracol*, the snail, because of the island's angular shape. On the western shore of the island is La Trinta Bay (ink), named by the Spanish for the black sand of its beaches, used to be a popular spot for smugglers and is now a popular sunbathing spot for Trinis on the weekend.

The Spaniards grew cotton on the island and established a whaling station and by the 1700's, Chacachacare had a sizable population. In the late 1700's, Chacachacare was given to an Irishman, Gerald Fitzpatrick Carry, for services rendered to the King with the proviso it would be returned if needed by the King. Carry took to growing sugar apples and cotton on the island.

In 1813, Venezuelan patriot Santiago Marino used Chacachacare as a base to launch an invasion of Venezuela during its war of independence. The ruins of Marino's house still stand on the point by Marino Bay.

In the 1800's, Chacachacare was used as a health spa and retreat for Trinidadians and then by the end of the 19th century this idyllic paradise was to change quite abruptly. In 1880, Dominican nuns built St. Catherine's Church, a school, and a convent on land that was willed to the Church in 1842. In 1896, a lighthouse was built on the island (Fl 10s, 824', 26M). Once the highest lighthouse in the world, it stands like a sentinel towering above

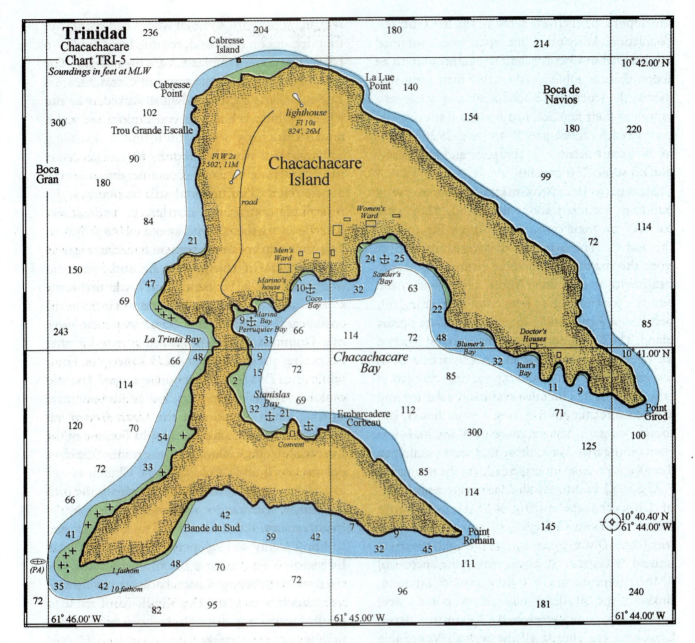

the surrounding waters. Today the lighthouse is the second highest lighthouse in the world, the highest lighthouse is now located in Russia. Today, the only full-time inhabitants of Chacachacare is the lightkeeper that lives in the century-old building atop the hill. In a way it's sad that the tradition of lighthouse keeping is quickly falling by the wayside around the world as more and more lights are turning to automatic operation. The lighthouse keeper on Chaca likes guests and stands by on VHF ch. 10, he'll often give visitors a ride to the lighthouse if he's not busy, but please don't bother him if you're just to lazy to take the short hike.

Chacachacare is best known for the leper colony that existed on the island for over half-a-century, or perhaps more. Dates are unclear concerning the timeline here. There has been speculation among Trinidadians that I have spoken with that the concept of a leper colony on Chacachacare was brought forth in the late 19th century, but remained dormant for almost 40 years. I have seen literature that states the leper colony was established on Chacachacare in 1877, while another reports the year as 1887. However, newspaper clippings from the early 20th century report that in the early 1920's the British government decided to separate the lepers of Trinidad from the rest of the population. At that time the lepers were contained at a hospital in Cocorite, and the authorities, in an action that resembled a raid rather than a transfer, moved the lepers to Chacachacare and the lepers, as well as their families, had no idea if they would ever see each other again. By the mid-1920's, most of the infrastructure was complete and the colony housed some 250 patients.

Most of the lepers lived in small groups in several buildings scattered about the island. They were basically on their own, including having to feed themselves. The Sisters used food shipped over from the mainland to induce patients to secure treatments at the clinic. Those lepers who could not care for themselves were confined to the 260-bed *Sunda Bay Hospital* in the small village on the island. The Dominican nuns, who unselfishly cared for the lepers, strictly forbid any contact between the sexes and as you would expect, this segregation raised a protest. The nuns eventually relented and allowed intermingling during certain hours, but things being as they are, more than one baby was born on the island, and those that were uninfected were transferred to an orphanage on the mainland.

U.S. and Puerto Rican Marines occupied part of Chacachacare during WW II, separating themselves from the leper colony with a barbed wire fence. During the war years the lighthouse was unused as German U-boats were quite successful in their hunting in the waters around Trinidad, sinking some 80 Allied ships. At one point a steel submarine net stretched westward from Chacachacare almost all the way to Venezuela across Boca Gran and the north entry to the Gulf of Paria. Chacachacare has always been a good source of fresh water and during the war years ships would pull in here to take on water. There are still the remains of viaducts and piping on the island.

In 1950, the Dominican nuns left the island and were replaced by a local nursing staff. Over the years, several of the Sisters died of the same disease as their patients and were buried in the cemetery on the island. Today, just up the hill from the convent, you can still visit the old graveyard where 12 nuns from age 28–88 are buried.

In 1984, the leper colony closed and the remaining patients, some of whom had spent over four decades on the island, returned to Trinidad to try to live some semblance of a normal life. The amazing thing about the ruins on Chacachacare is that it looks as if everybody just walked away and left everything behind. As you explore the wards and the doctor's house you'll find desks, filing cabinets with patients records, part of an X-ray machine with a patient's X-rays nearby, and even a typewriter. The hospital still has beds and a pharmacy containing bottles of medication. There's even a theater with an old movie projector. You can't help but wonder as you stand there staring at the mass of things left behind, why did everybody just leave like that? It's said that some of the buildings are haunted, and writings on the walls bear testament to this. Some say it's the ghost of a Dominican nun who took her own life after becoming pregnant by a local fisherman For a while the *Trinidad Coast Guard* used the old buildings for living quarters and as administrative offices, but it is said that the *Coast Guard* left Chacachacare after only six months because of the haunted buildings. Along with the ruins of the leper colony, you'll find an old Catholic Church as well as a Hindu temple. And don't just stay to the path or road, if you wander around in the brush you might be surprised at what you'll find. Don't forget to bring plenty of bug spray, the mosquitoes can be vicious. There are a lot of caves along the northwestern shore of Chacachacare that were used by smugglers for years. One gentleman I spoke to recalled wandering through the caves as a boy and finding a case of whiskey.

Today the island is overseen by the *CDA*, the *Chaguaramas Development Authority*, and they have proposed constructing hotels on the island as well as preserving the remains of the leper colony. As of this writing, nothing has progressed on this action.

As shown on Chart TRI-2, a GPS waypoint at 10° 43.00' N, 61° 44.35' W, will place you approximately 1 mile north of *Boca de Navios*, the passage between Huevos Island and Chacachacare. Pass between the two in deep water and after passing south of Point Girod you can turn to the west to anchor in one of the small bays off

Chacachacare Bay as shown on Chart TRI-5. These anchorages are exposed to the southeast, but Stanislas Bay, and especially Sanders Bay, give the best protection from that direction. Unfortunately the bays here are deep and shelve rapidly, and if that's not enough, the holding is generally fair to poor and the bottom rocky. It's best to set an anchor and run a line ashore.

The island is wonderful to explore, but caution must be exercised, as there are *Manchineel* trees growing on the island. If you are not familiar with *Manchineel* trees, learn about them. Their sap is toxic and it's inadvisable to even stand underneath one, especially if it is raining. A hint...the *Manchineel* and its fruit resembles an apple tree. Luckily for you however, they tend to congregate close to the water and not far inland...but keep your eyes open for them.

And what will you visit while ashore? Yes of course, the leper colony ruins, but other treasures also await you (see Chart TRI-5). Trek to the operating lighthouse for a fantastic view of Trinidad and Venezuela. But if your visit to the lighthouse is not enough, visit the salt pond at the southwestern tip of the island at Bande du Sud. Divers might wish to explore the waters around Bolo Rocks where three wrecks are reported to lie, the *Samuel* in 1809, the *Pirata* in 1892, and the *Dr. Sigert* in 1895.

■ THE WESTERN COAST OF TRINIDAD

Chaguaramas Bay

This is it, the Mecca of Caribbean cruising. Cruise central. At the end of the 1980's, the only place in Trinidad for a cruiser to get a slip and spend the season, was at *TTYC*, the *Trinidad and Tobago Yacht Club* in Bayshore. Over the last decade Chaguaramas has literally burst forth into the center of marine services in the lower Caribbean,

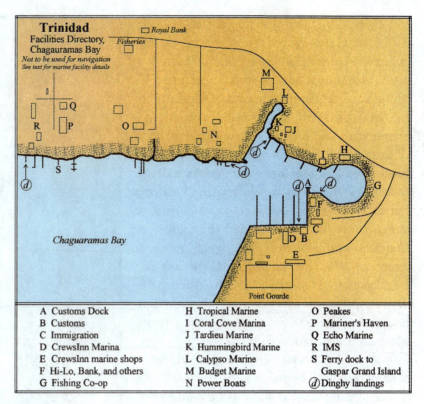

the fastest growing marine industry in the Caribbean. You can probably find anything you need here, and if you can't, you can get it shipped in with no duty. Chaguaramas, being technically out of the hurricane zone, is a huge draw for vessels wishing not to deal with hurricanes and yet still enjoy the Caribbean and the camaraderie of other like-minded cruisers.

The peninsula was named Chaguaramas by its original Amerindian inhabitants (100–700A.D.), after the majestic Royal palms which once flourished here. This natural harbor has been favored for its depth and shelter for centuries. Chaguaramas Bay offered sheltered moorings for Spanish, French, and British ships, which fought over Trinidad for over two hundred years. The Spaniards burned their fleet here when the British invaded in 1797. During the plantation years, the area saw coffee, cocoa, and cotton estates worked by slave labor and later by indentured servants. World War II saw the area leased to the American military in exchange for 50 old destroyers as part of the *Lend-Lease Program*. During this period the area was closed to all civilians, and the inhabitants were moved to what is now Carenage. Today, most of the large buildings you see, especially those that line the road from *TTSA* to Carenage, were constructed for military use during the war years.

As the independence movement grew in Trinidad, Chaguaramas became a focal point. In April of 1960, thousands of residents marched in the rain to solicit the return of Chaguaramas to the people of Trinidad. The beaches of Chaguaramas were always a draw, and in 1961 the area was returned to the citizens and the Government of Trinidad immediately set aside most of the region as *Chaguaramas National Park*, which remains today. In 1962 the *CDA*, the *Chaguaramas Development Authority* was established with the purpose of maintaining the natural resources of the area and encourage the growth of a business infrastructure.

Today, the town of Chaguaramas is the area of large buildings between *TTSA* and eastward to *KFC*. The *CDA* is located here and they offer guides and hikes through the surrounding area such as the hike through the Tucker Estate, the first citrus plantation on Trinidad. The Covigne River tour is a hike through a majestic gorge ending up at a waterfall with a deep pool at its base, perfect for a cool dip after the hike. Birdwatchers will appreciate the hike to Mount Catherine, and everybody will enjoy the tour to Edith Falls. Edith Falls can be arrived at by road as well if you prefer to go on your own in a rental car. Take the Tucker Valley Road to the well-marked turn-off to the Falls at Bellerazand Road. There is a small and poorly-marked trail just before the Golf Course and Edith Falls a short 30 minute hike away, awaits patiently for you. If you wish to camp, *CDA* will rent a tent to you for your stay.

The entrance to Chaguaramas Bay really doesn't need a waypoint, as you approach from the north, through the first Boca (Boca de Monos-Chart TRI-2), but if you need one I'll be happy to give you one. A waypoint at 10° 40.50' N, 61° 40.00' W, will place you 1½ miles west of the anchorage area as shown on Chart TRI-6. If you don't need a waypoint, as you head south in the Boca you'll pass Cannings

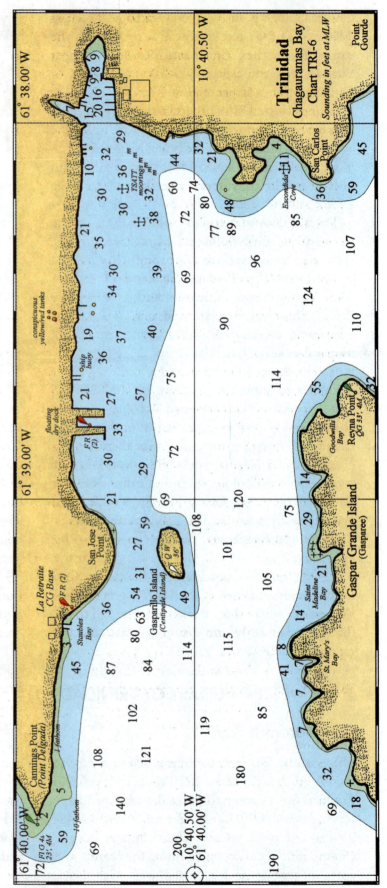

Point at which point you can turn to port to pass either side of Gasparillo Island to proceed to the anchorage west of *Crews Inn Marina*. On most charts Cannings Point is called Point Delgada, or Delgada Point. Either way, it is known locally as Cannings Point and that's good enough for me, so that's what I'll show it as. Keep an eye out for the submerged rock just off the point. Called Teteron Rock, it is marked by a lit buoy, but if the light should not be on station, give the point a wide berth, at least ¼ mile, to be on the safe side. Just before Teteron Rock you'll notice Teteron Bay, the home of the *Trinidad and Tobago Naval Station*. The bay is restricted and anchoring is not permitted. Gasparillo Island is known locally as Centipede Island for the huge centipede population that controls the island. The largest centipede ever captured, 14", was caught on Gaparillo Island.

The anchorage in Chaguaramas is deep, usually 25'–30' and more, the holding isn't the best, and the area is beset with currents. You'll soon notice that your boat will swing to the swirling currents and vessels nudging into each other at these times is not unusual. Keep a good anchor watch and try to give yourself enough swinging room. Do not anchor close to the large shipwright's building at *Crews Inn*, or close along the southern shore below *Peake's, Power Boats,* and *Humming Bird Marinas.*

YSATT now has moorings in Chaguaramas Bay, a good idea as anyone can tell you. The moorings lie west of the *Crews Inn* docks stretching westward. The large red floats are easy to see with *YSATT* painted on them and *YSATT* has plans to place several more of these in the future. If you wish to rent one, pick up a vacant mooring and check in at the *YSATT* office at *Crews Inn Marina*. The moorings are understandably on a first-come/first-served basis.

Vessels needing to clear in should continue past the *Crews Inn* docks to the *Customs* dock, which can usually accommodate two, and sometimes three, vessels. Although some cruisers will anchor first and then dinghy in to clear, *Customs* officers frown on this practice, they would appreciate your tying up to their dock as is expected. After you tie up to the dock, walk down the first row of boats and at the end of the dock, walk up the stairs and to your left are the steps leading up to the *Immigration* office, your first stop. When you have cleared with *Immigration*, walk down the stairs and just off to your right is the *Customs* office, your next stop. When you have completed your clearing-in process proceed to the marina of your choice or anchor wherever you choose. Vessels heading to *TTYC* can tie up there and then take a maxi-taxi to *Crews Inn* to clear *Customs* and *Immigration*.

There are several marinas available here and they might be full so give them a call on the VHF to check on slip availability. Most monitor VHF ch. 68 and have dinghy docks available (some offer use of their facilities for a small weekly fee). The facilities at *TTYC* in Bayshore, and *TTSA* in Carenage Bay will be discussed in upcoming sections so if you wish to leave Chaguaramas Bay for those locations, turn to their appropriate section for more information and approach directions. We will now explore each marina and what marine services are available. Check the appendix in the back for phone numbers and e-mail addresses. Bear in mind time changes all and by the time this publication reaches your hands, several of these businesses may have changed, moved, or closed. The *Chaguaramas Facilities Directory* map will give you a general idea of where some of these services are located around the periphery of Chaguaramas Bay. Another good source of information is the free *Trinidad and Tobago Boater's Directory*, available for free at all marinas, chandlers, and at the *Boca* offices and *YSATT*. Now let's see what marinas, haul-out yards, and marine services are available. We'll start by the *Custom's* dock and work our way counter-clockwise around the periphery of Chaguaramas Bay.

Our first stop is *CrewInn Marina*, a great place to stay, and definitely the most upscale of the marinas in Chaguaramas. The marina monitors VHF ch. 68 and 77 and there's usually somebody around 24/7. The docks have over 60 slips with finger piers (rare in Caribbean marinas), and full electric (metered) with water, cable TV, and a daily newspaper in your cockpit every morning. Marina guests also have access to the showers, laundry, and

Crew's Inn Marina, Chaguaramas, Trinidad.

pool at the *Crews Inn Hotel*. On the ground floor by the *Customs* dock is a *Hi-Lo* supermarket (Mon-Sat, 9–9, Sun. 8–Noon) with an excellent choice of foodstuffs, fresh produce, and spirits. Above the supermarket is the *Lighthouse Restaurant*, a great place to eat and/or drink with good prices and a great view of Chaguaramas Bay. Below the restaurant by A-dock is the *Mariner's Office* where you can access the Internet, send and receive faxes, ship and receive packages, and make phone calls at good prices. Just past the *Mariner's Office* is a spirituous beverage store and a video rental. Up the stairs at the end of A-dock is *Customs* and *Immigration* as mentioned earlier. If you take a left and walk up the steps past the *Mariner's Office* you'll come to a nice courtyard (this area is called the *Crews Inn Village Square*) the location for Thursday night pot-lucks. Bring something to grill and have a good time. Take a right here and walk up a few steps and you'll find a gift shop as well as *Econo Car* car rentals, great prices, only TT$90 per day. Here too you'll find *YSATT*, *SOS* style shop, and *Trump Tours*. Behind *Econo Car*, facing the parking lot, is a *Republic Bank* with a 24-hour *ATM*.

Across from the hotel office, the *Quarterdeck* (with a nice reading room for marina guests), is a long building with several marine services. *Nau-T-Kol* can handle your marine refrigeration and air-conditioning problems, while *Soca Sails* can repair your sails, or build you a new one, and they're reps for *Doyle Sails*. *Dockyard Electrics* has just expanded and carries all your electrical needs from wire crimps to batteries and solar panels. They will not only sell you the best of electrical systems, they'll install it for you or repair your old system. *Goodwood Marine* has a new shop here and they sell and service marine electronics as well as roller-furling systems and winches.

Just behind these shops is the huge shipwright's building, part of the old Navy base, that is the focus for the *Crews Inn* 4-acre haul-out yard. The building itself covers 2½ acres and has a vertical clearance of 80' so you won't have to pull your mast for inside painting (unless of course, your mast is too tall for this immense building). The yard can handle the largest yachts with a 200-ton lift as well as a 65-ton crane.

Security is very good here, 24 hours a day, and the guards even check car's trunks upon entry into the yard. And just because you get in the yard, doesn't mean you can get into the shipwright's building where another gate and guard will stop you. As of this writing, the marina is phasing the marine hoist operation to commercial usage.

As you round the eastern end of Chaguaramas Bay you'll pass the small cove full of local fishing cove. There is a fishing co-op here and no facilities for yachts.

As you proceed west on the Western Main Road you'll immediately come to *Tropical Marine*. Here you'll find stern or bow-to berthing for about 20 or so boats, depending on their beam The boats are very close together and fenders will be required to keep you away from your neighbor. Water and electricity are available and the slips are very economical. Call ahead for a slip as *Tropical* seems to stay full.

Fronting the road is a building housing several facilities including *Master's Laundry* where you can wash your clothes or have it done for you. There is also a book swap. Facing the road as well is *Electropics* where you can get just about any electronic device on your boat repaired, including autopilots. They are an authorized *Simrad* dealer and repair center. *KISS* offers their own brand of high output wind-generators at a low price, check them out, you might be pleasantly surprised. *Yacht Maintenance and Repair* specializes in sandblasting, re-galvanizing, the general maintenance of yachts, and corrosion problems. *Coastal Diving Services, Ltd.* can fill your SCUBA tank, and if you need a car, *Convenient Car Rental* is on the south side of the building facing the dock. Also in back is *Shiloh Enterprises* where you can pick up bulk fiberglass cloth, resins, and epoxies. The *Wheelhouse Pub* is a popular hangout with pool tables and live music on occasion.

Next door is *Coral Cove Marina*, a large haul-out facility with a 60-ton lift and long-term dry storage. The marina can handle about 60 boats (up to a 90' monohull and wide slips for catamarans) with full electric, water, laundry, and cable TV. The *Coral Cove Marina Hotel* can furnish a room if you need someplace to stay while you're hauled out. Next door is *Tardieu Marine*, which we'll discuss in just a moment, but first let's talk about the building facing Western Main Road that stretches between the two. In it you'll find the best pizza parlor around, *Joe's*, great pizza and Italian foods, a must for the visiting cruiser. At the other end of the building is the *Curry Bien Restaurant* serving breakfast and lunch. Located between the two restaurants you'll find *Sigma Coatings* for your painting needs. *Marine Shop, Ltd.* has a good supply of marine related goods and *C.E. Tang Yuk & Co.* sometimes called *Caribbean Ropes*, handles *Sea Recovery* watermakers, *Lugger* marine diesel generators, and carries marine electrical supplies and accessories. *SGI Distributors, Ltd.* sells tools, *Diehard* batteries, and plumbing supplies. *William H. Scott, Ltd.* also sells as well as rents power tools and carries miscellaneous hardware supplies. *Navtech Electronics* handles marine navigational electronics and *Trinidad Detroit Diesel* can service or install *Cummins*, *Perkins*, and *Caterpillar* engines.

At the eastern end of this building is the entrance to the facilities at *Tardieu Marine*. The office for the marina is on the upper floor in the last building on the left before the dock. The two rows of buildings at *Tardieu* house some of the best marine services in Chaguaramas. *Webster's Canvas* and *Alpha Canvas* both handle canvas and upholstery work. *Gittens Engine Service* repairs outboards and diesel while *Engines Engines* also handles engines and outboards as well transmissions. *Marine Warehouse* is a popular chandlery though they don't have large stock, their forte is ordering what you need from wherever it originates at prices to compete with the largest marine chains such as *West Marine* or *Boat/US*. Lincoln at *Chaguaramas Metal* works can fabricate whatever you need in aluminum or stainless steel and creates some really nice arches. *Caribbean Propellers* is the place to go for prop and shaft repairs or repalcement. Sherrie at *Sherrie's Laundry*, besides doing your laundry, can make you a new shirt or shorts, just bring here the material or see what she's got available. Next to Sherrie's is an excellent woodworking shop that repairs and constructs whatever you need. They made me a very nice teak wheel adapter for a wind vane and at a very nice price. *Corsa Marketing* handles *Mercury* and *Mariner* parts, service, and sales. *Barrow Sails* has an workshop here for the construction of frames and arches, and they can also weld stainless and aluminum for you. The guys here are very knowledgeable, friendly, and fast. *Ocean Internet Cafe* has an office here as well.

Next to *Tardieu* is the entrance to the *Humming Bird Marina/Stella Maris* compound where you'll find *Voyager's Restaurant*. You've got to stop here and see the collection of memorabilia of ocean voyagers including Harold LaBord, the well-known Trini circumnavigator. Writers will be interested in attending the Wednesday writer's meetings at the *Voyager* from 1000–1200. *Voyager's* has excellent soups for lunch and occasional pot-lucks. *Humming Bird* has alongside berths as well as bow or stern-to berths, water, electricity, showers, and a laundry. They can accommodate up to 24 boats depending on their beam and length.

At the end of the little cove next to *Humming Bird* is *Calypso Marine Services, Ltd.* The guys here build some very nice fiberglass pirogues that people come from all over Trinidad, Tobago, and the Windwards to purchase. They can help you with fiberglass and outboard repairs.

A hundred yards to the west is the large *Budget Marine* store, a place all cruisers come to know and love. A very well-stocked chandlery, this *Budget* is second in size only to their huge store in Simpson Bay, Saint Maarten. *Budget* also sells *Mercury* outboards and the *Budget Marine Rigging* shop has a very good selection of rigging hardware and can handle any rigging problem you might have from swaging to splicing.

Next door is the huge *Power Boats* complex, and no, it's name does not imply that it is for power boats, 99% of *Power Boats* customers are sailboats. *Power Boats* has a fuel dock with diesel and gas, two dozen slips with bow or stern-to berthing and full amenities. The yard itself is huge, with space for about 200 boats and it stays quite full, you might wish to make arrangements well in advance to assure that there's room for your haulout.

There's a 50-ton lift and the yard can also handle large catamarans. *Sail's Restaurant* is the local hangout and offers live entertainment on most Friday nights. Next to *Sails* is the newly opened well-stocked *Dockside Market* grocery store. Just up from the fuel dock is a small yellow trailer where you'll find *Mega Books on Wheels*, where you can buy or trade reading material. Just in from the dinghy dock by the lift area you'll see a flight of stairs that will take you up to the *Ocean Internet Cafe* where you can check your e-mail and surf the net to your heart's content. *Hull Support*, the small blue building well hidden west of the much larger blue building which houses the offices, laundromat, and showers, can fill your dive tanks for you. At the northeastern end of the compound is a large two story building which houses *Fortress Woodworking*, whose name implies their field of expertise, and *Awon's Marine*, who can handle wood refinishing and gelcoat problems. Next door is a small shop set up for the yachties to work on their projects. Here you'll find tables, electricity, and a vise. The *Boater's Shop*, a small chandlery is next door while *Caribbean Marine* are electrical,

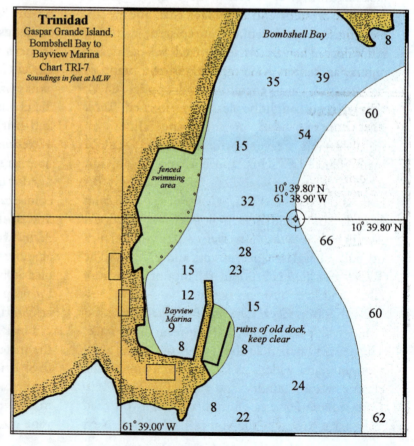

battery, and diesel injector specialists. Also on site is *Barrow Sails*, *Mark's Car Rentals*, *The Upholstery Shop*, and the *Rainbow Company* for hull painting.

Further west is the large *Peake's* yard with a large 150-ton lift that can handles yachts with beams up to 27½' and drafts to 15'. A unique trailer can pack about 300 boats in the yard. The waterfront can accommodate up to 17 boats with bow or stern-to berthing, less berths depending on beam, catamarans taking up more dock space than monohulls. *The Bight* is a small hotel if you need a room while you're hauled out. *Ocean Internet Cafe* has an office here and *The Bight* restaurant is a very popular hangout for cruisers. In the main building is the *Thomas Peake Chandlery*, a well-stocked marine supply store that also handles *Johnson* outboard repairs and parts. *Antoines Woodworking* and *John Francois Woodworking* can remedy all your wood and shipwright problems. Antoine's can also handle *Awlgrip* painting. *KNJ Marine Service* can help you with your painting, varnishing, and general maintenance needs. *Fluid Hose and Coupling* is a great spot if you need hydraulic, fuel, air, and exhaust hoses or fittings.

At the western end of *Peake's* is their covered painting facility as well as *Billy's Rigging*. Owner Bill Wray can handle all the normal types of rigging repairs as well as rod rigging and the x-ray of fittings, and can provide *Lloyd's* approved surveys. Also located here are *Ali's Machine Shop* that can weld and fabricate whatever you need in stainless and aluminum. *Propeller and Marine Service* can handle prop and shaft repairs, as well as stainless and aluminum welding. *Cask Woodworking* is there for your wood repairs or fabrication and can repair decks as well. *Serge's Electrical* can handle electrical and generator repairs and battery installation. *Convenient Car Rental* is located here along with a small store and the *Sail and Fly Travel Agency*. *Calypso Marine Canvas* is located here as is *Carlos' Marine Electronics*.

Just west of *Peake's* on the north side of the Western Main Road is the *Royal Bank* with its 24-hour *ATM*. On the south side of the road is the *Caribbean Fisheries Training and Development Institute*. Proceeding westward you'll pass several commercial marine businesses and storage tanks before coming to the *Mariner's Haven* and *IMS* complexes.

Mariner's Haven is the new kid on the block and by the time this guide is published is scheduled to have a new commercial dry dock in place. You will know when you have located their facility, they're fronted on the road by a large concrete wall topped with concertina wire. You'll find a lot of marine services located here including *Echo Marine*, the place to go for solar panels, watermakers, electronic navigation instruments, dinghies, paint, generators, refrigeration systems, and oodles and oodles of accessories. *Echo Marine* also has a stainless steel and aluminum workshop on site. *Marc One Marine Supplies* handles everything from fiberglass supplies to inverters, power tools, and fuel filters, and they deliver. *Maharaj Electrical* is your stop here for electrical supplies while *Island Surf Cafe* is the place to go for Internet access here, they also carry a good selection of computer accessories. Also on site are *International Tubular Services*, *Fiber Tech*, *Delta Logistics*, *Caribbean Workshops*, and *Caribbean Welders*.

Next door is the *IMS* compound, *Industrial Marine Services*. The boatyard has a capacity of approximately 130 boats, a 70-ton lift, and their slips offer free electricity and water as well as the usual showers and laundry (not free). The popular

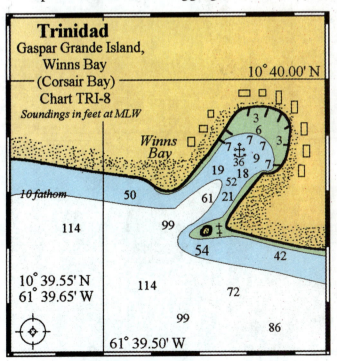

Galley Restaurant serves breakfast, lunch, and dinner with happy hours every Friday at 1700 and the occasional movie on Thursdays at 1900. *IMS* manufactures their own brand of paint, for more info speak to Glenn in the office.

Located in the *IMS* complex are *Atlantic Yacht Services* who can coordinate repairs for your vessel as well as rent you the tools to do it yourself if that is more to your liking. *Ocean Sails* has a large loft here to handle construction and repairs of all sails. Also on site you'll find *Dynamite*, a yacht management and delivery service. If you wish to leave your boat here long-term, talk to them about shrink-warp protection. *Sign Lab* can paint the name of your vessel on your hull or supply you with a stencil or graphic decal. *Unity Metals* fabricates in stainless and aluminum, and *Diesel Technology* repairs all makes of diesel engines.

Next to *IMS* is the ferry dock where you can catch the water taxi to Gaspar Grande Island while west of IMS are only commercial facilities all the way to the end of the road where you find the entrance to the *TT Coast Guard* and *Naval Stations*.

At the northwestern end of the bay, just northeast of Gasparillo Island, is a huge floating drydock. The dock itself was built on the Tyne by the famous Newcastle firm of *Swan, Hunter and Wigan Richardson*, and was towed to Trinidad by Dutch tugs in 1907. The dock can accommodate a vessel 365' long and up to 64' wide, with a capacity of 4,800 tons.

Gaspar Grande

Gaspar Grand Island, sometimes called Gasparee, originally belonged to Don Gaspar de Percin, hence its name. Governor Chacon once built forts on the island to defend the island as a last stand, in fact, you can view the remains of one of them at Bombshell Bay. *Fort Apodaca*, sits atop the hill above Point Baleine. It was named after the Spanish commander of the fleet who was sent to protect Trinidad. When the Spaniards surrendered in 1797, Gaspar Grande was the focus of a lengthy dispute over which country, Spain or England, actually owned the island. Shortly thereafter a whaling station was

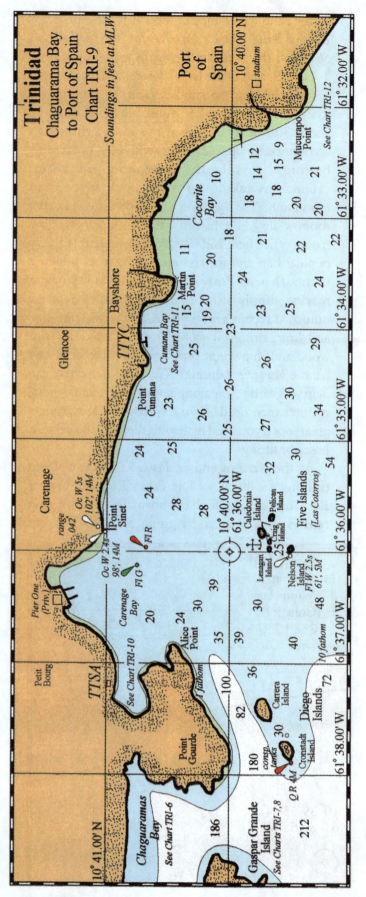

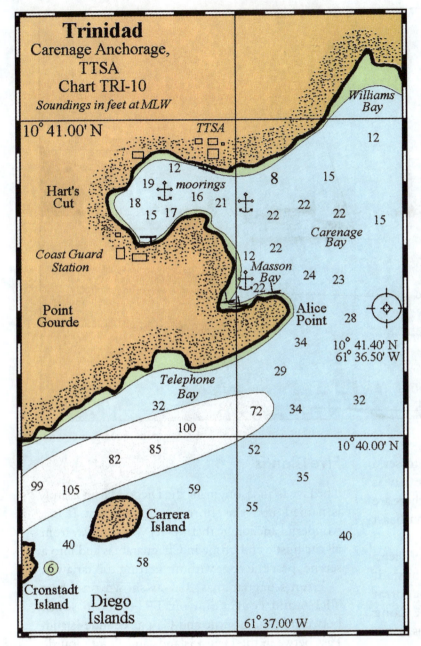

bats. At high tide the caves fill with seawater. There are free water-taxi rides to Gaspar Grande Island leaving the dock by *IMS* (see *Facilities Directory*) that run about every two hours. For special occasions you can catch a water taxi from *Power Boats* and *Crew's Inn* as well.

On the eastern shore of Gaspar Grande Island, just south of Bombshell Bay (as shown on Chart TRI-7), you'll find the *Bay View Beach Resort and Marina*, once called *Fantasy Island*. A GPS waypoint at 10° 39.80' N, 61° 39.80' W, will place you approximately .1 of a mile northeast of the entrance to the marina. Head into towards the beach and turn to port keeping the end of the jetty to port. The beach is fenced off and the entrance may appear narrower than it really is. Dockage is stern or bow-to and you must call ahead for a slip assignment on VHF ch. 68. The marina can accommodate approximately 12 vessels.

Today the marina area appears a bit rundown since its earlier days as *Fantasy Island*, but it is planning on improvements. As of this writing there is water and electricity available, showers, laundry, swimming pool, cable TV and a restaurant and bar.

Heading to the southern shore of Gaspar Grande Island, you'll find Winn's Bay, a pleasant anchorage marked by a large fig tree situated on the small rock lying off the point. As shown on Chart TRI-8, a GPS waypoint at 10° 39.55' N, 61° 39.65' W, will place you approximately ¼ mile southwest of the entrance. Head in towards the bay between the off-lying rock and the point of land to the west of it. The rock is very conspicuous, there is a small stand of fig trees on the rock, and on weekends there's usually a dozen or so people on the rock fishing.

The water will shallow towards the northern end of the bay so don't head too far in, keep an eye on the depthsounder. The wind can be fluky here, as in so many of the anchorages in Trinidad, especially the ones along the northern coast with their

established on Gaspar Grande, and later cotton was grown here. There was an old guesthouse at Point Baleine at the western tip of the island where Noel Coward wrote his novel *Point Valeine*. Point Baleine was once home to a whaling station.

Today the island is home to several vacation homes and visitors can explore the *Gasparee Caves* at Point Baleine, said to have once been used by pirates. Walk up the path from the jetty to the white and yellow house where you'll find a guide. Once inside the cave, steps lead down into a cavern where you'll see stalagmites, stalactites, and fruit

Moorings at TTSA, Carenage, Trinidad.

surrounding mountains. You might wish to set a second anchor or set a line ashore. The bay is surrounded by several vacation homes and there are no facilities ashore here. In moderate southeast winds it can get bit rolly in here.

South of Gaspar Grande Island are The Diego Islands (TRI-9), Carrera Island and Cronstadt Island (sometimes called Creteau or Begorrat Island), which were once known as the Long Islands, a holiday resort. Cronstadt Island is now a bayrite ore production station (bayrite ore is a product needed in the oilfields). The ore is brought in and crushed and stored on the island before shipping out. Carrera Island is a hard-labor prison that was originally constructed in 1877. Like San Francisco's legendary Alcatraz, it is claimed that nobody has escaped from Carrera Island.

If you'd care to check your compass, you'll be happy to know that you can do it just off Gaspar Grande Island. Line up the light at Point Baleine on the western tip of Gaspar Grande and the light on Teteron Rock off Cannings Point, and that line will be true north.

Five Islands

The Five Islands, originally the Diego Martin Islands is named after the shoreside community. It is a wonderful anchorage that will let you get away from all the hustle and bustle in Chaguaramas and into a serene, peaceful spot without getting too far away.

From Chaguaramas Bay, as shown on Chart TRI-6 and continuing on TRI-9, head south between Point Gourde and Gaspar Grande Island. Pass between the Diego Islands and Point Gourde (TRI-9) and make your way to a GPS waypoint at 10° 40.00'N, 61° 36.00' W, which places you approximately ¼ mile north/northwest of the Five Islands. Simply head in toward Caledonia Island and anchor in the lee of the islands wherever your draft allows and you feel comfortable.

Nelson Island, sometimes called Neilson's Island, is Trinidad's version of Ellis Island in New York. Between 1845 and 1917, thousands of East Indians were kept on Nelson Island before beginning their indenture on the sugar plantations of Trinidad. Nearby Pelican Island and Rock

Island, the small islet just west of Nelson Island, were quarantine stations. The islands are great for exploring with small concrete buildings here and there, and steps leading into the interior of the islands.

Most charts show a shallow area labeled *Foul* lying approximately 1½ miles southwest of Five Islands. I'm told by a former member of a marine rescue unit, of having to pull several boats off a shallow rock approximately ½ mile south/southwest of the Five Islands. I have not been able to find this rock, perhaps it is indeed that *Foul* area, perhaps not, but if you traverse the area west-south of Five Islands, use the utmost caution.

Carenage Bay and TTSA

The moorings at the *Trinidad Tobago Sailing Association* (*TTSA*) are a popular spot for cruisers. You'll be away from Chaguaramas in a small bay with little traffic, and yet you're only a short walk away from the facilities surrounding Chaguaramas Bay. Carenage Bay, and the small town of the same name, were named for the fact that Spanish captains would careen their ships here so that the crews could scrape their bottoms. The settlement of Carenage almost became a ghost town after the Spanish departed in 1797. When the Americans arrive during WW II and claimed the Chaguaramas peninsula, the residents there were relocated to Carenage when the town earned a seedy reputation thanks to the servicemen that came there for rum and women.

From Chaguaramas Bay, as shown on Chart TRI-6 and continuing on TRI-9, head south between Point Gourde and Gaspar Grande Island. Keeping between the Diego Islands and Point Gourde (TRI-9), follow the shoreline to Alice Point to a waypoint shown on Chart TRI-10, a GPS waypoint at 10° 41.40.00'N, 61° 36.50' W, places you approximately ½ mile southeast of the mooring field off *TTSA*. If you don't care to pick up a mooring, you can anchor southeast of the fleet of moored boats, or behind them, between the mooring field and the beach on the mainland. Several boats can often be seen anchored in Masson Bay, thought there's sometimes a barge anchored against the shore.

TTSA is for sailboats only and the moorings cost (at the time of this writing), US$1 per foot a week with a one week minimum which will allow you use of the facilities as well as water that you'll either have to jerry-jug or tie up to the dock briefly to fill up with a hose. When the wind goes into the southeast and picks up it gets a bit choppy in the Carenage, nothing really dangerous, just uncomfortable, however if the wind were to be forecast as extremely strong, I'd certainly move to Five Islands or back to Chaguaramas Bay.

TTSA is home to the *Spinnaker Bar and Restaurant*, a popular yachtie hangout with Monday night pot-lucks, weekly Trivia contests, and occasional movie nights. There is also a sailing school here and a pool that is restricted to use by children. *TTSA* has a haul out facility with a 35-ton lift and long term dry storage if you care to leave your boat here while you return home for a while. This is one of the safest yards in the Chaguaramas area. Boaters with projects have the use of the *TTSA* workshop.

In the small cove at the head of the bay is the *Trinidad and Tobago Coast Guard Station*. The CG dock may look like a small marina, but rest assured it is private. The long building on shore at the head of the bay is the *Anchorage Restaurant*. Hart's Cut, named after a police superintendent named Hart, was created in the 1856 to link Carenage to Chaguaramas Bay and was 15' wide and only 4' deep. This cut was designed for Trinidadian fisherman, saving them the long row to windward around Point Gourde

If you walk out onto the road and take a left, you'll come to the Chaguaramas Bay area with all of its amenities. If you don't feel like walking, catch a maxi-taxi. If you take a right on the road you'll soon come to a large building on the water that has plans to become a major haul-out yard, and may even be so by the time this book is published. As of this moment there are only a few commercial and naval vessels hauled out for repairs. Across the street is *Aikane*, a local company that builds quality catamarans as well as offering dry storage for cats. A few steps down the road, and across from *Aikane*, is the *Chaguaramas Military History and Aviation Museum*, a very interesting place, where you'll learn of Trinidad's role in the wars of the 20th century. Inside you'll discover that during WW II over 80 allied ships were sunk off Trinidad by German U-boats, that Chaguaramas had a submarine net stretched across its entrance, and that there were numerous Allied bases on the island during the war years. Besides the military relics and exhibits, the museum also offers historical data on the British years on the island, the history of the Trinidad police, and even pirates are mentioned here.

Across the Western Main Road is *Bowen Marine*, a huge building, where you can have your outboard repaired. All of these buildings that you see here are old Naval facilities dating back World War II. Next to *Bowen Marine* is the *Chaguaramas Hotel and Convention Center*, a rebuilt WW II military barracks, with an Internet access site called *SameSame*. On the road behind the hotel you'll find *Marine Safety Equipment* where you can get your liferaft serviced or purchase a new one. They carry an Irish-made design that is of very good quality and very economical. Continuing down the road you'll come to a *KFC* as well as several little food stalls selling good homemade local dishes. Further down the road is *Pier One*, once a nice marina, but now closed, it's private and is basically a party place.

Cumana Bay and TTYC

As shown on Chart TRI-9, and in detail on Chart TRI-11, Cumana Bay and the *Trinidad and Tobago Yacht Club* (*TTYC*), offer a very good alternative to Chaguaramas Bay. In fact, before the explosion of marine facilities in Chaguaramas Bay, *TTYC* was the only place around for visiting yachts, it's been in existence for over 40 years.

From Chaguaramas, as shown on Chart TRI-6 and continuing on TRI-9, head south between Point Gourde and Gaspar Grande Island. Then pass between Carrera Island and Point Gourde (TRI-9) and take up a heading of approximately 95° to a GPS waypoint at 10° 40.40' N, 61° 34.30' W (TRI-11), which will place you approximately ¼ mile south/southwest of *TTYC* in Cumana Bay. From the waypoint head in towards the jetty and anchor either south or southeast of the jetty. If you are planning to get a slip at *TTYC*, give them a call on VHF 68 for directions. If you wish to fill-up with fuel, the fuel dock is on the western side of the main dock by the red-roofed restaurant. Use caution entering here though as the shallows stretch out a good distance from shore, but drafts of 6' and less should not have a problem. A good landmark to help you find *TTYC* is the orange and white striped tower with a fixed red light atop sitting just behind *TTYC*.

TTYC has diesel and gas, slips for US$15 per day or US$375 per month, which includes water, electricity, and cable TV. Getting a slip makes you

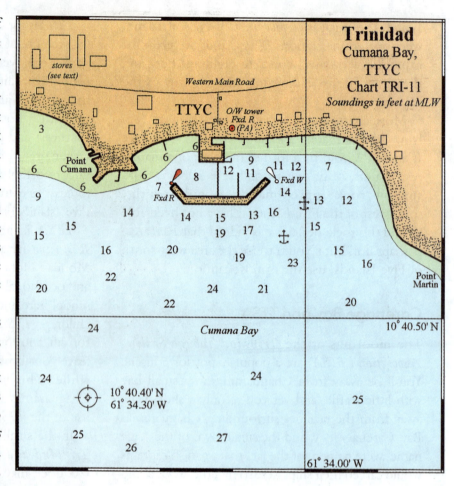

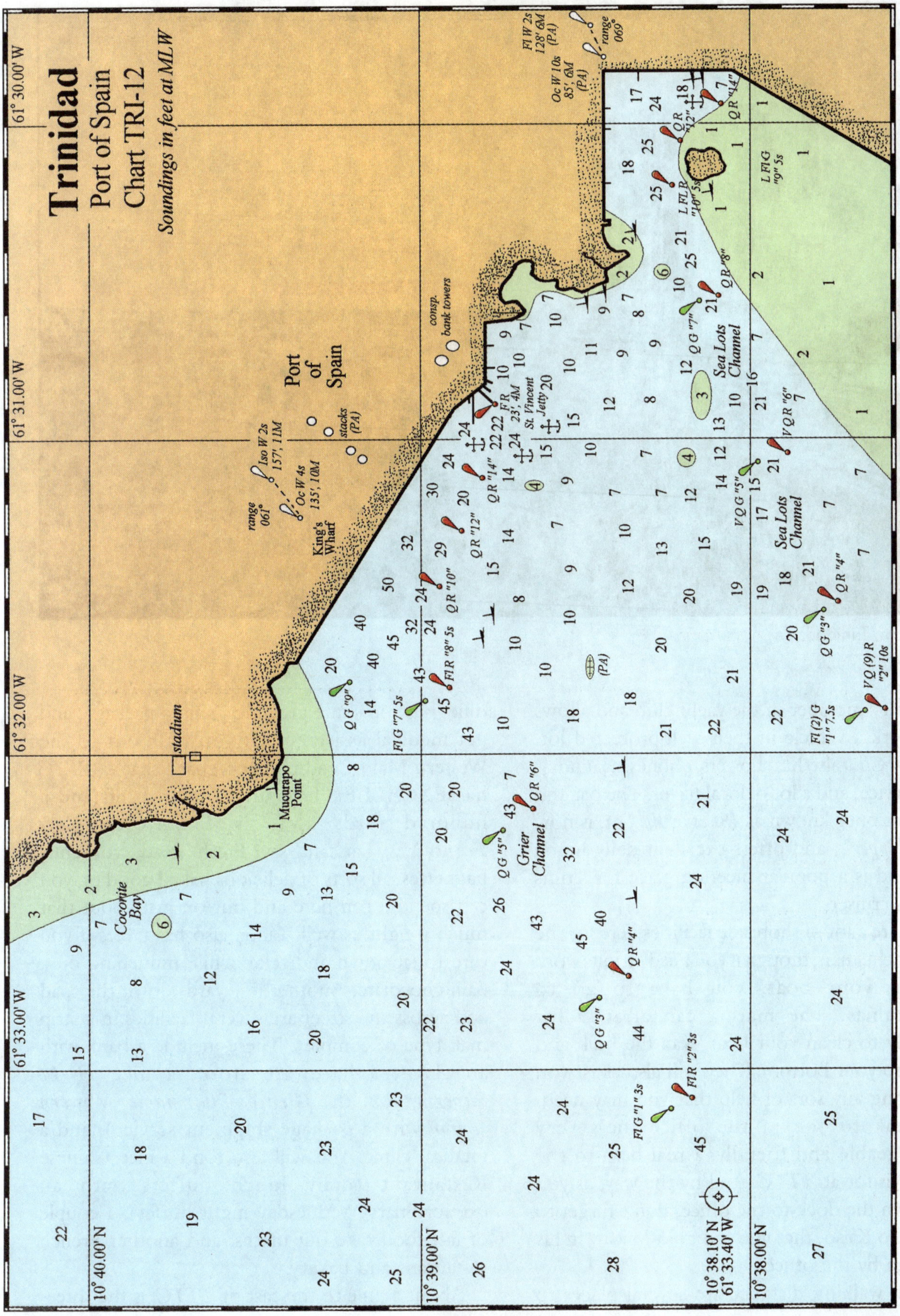
Trinidad
Port of Spain
Chart TRI-12
Soundings in feet at MLW
Port of Spain
King's Wharf
St. Vincent Jetty
Mucurapo Point
Cocorite Bay
stadium
Grier Channel
Sea Lots Channel
consp. bank towers
stacks (PA)
61° 30.00' W
61° 31.00' W
61° 32.00' W
61° 33.00' W
10° 40.00' N
10° 39.00' N
10° 38.00' N
10° 38.10' N 61° 33.40' W

Port of Spain, Trinidad.

a temporary member of the yacht club and allows you to park a vehicle in their well-protected lot. The *Yacht Club* also has showers, phones, a laundry, e-mail service, and a lot of local flavor. The bar and restaurant, once known as *Pisces by the Sea*, is now called *Skipper's*, and offers excellent daily lunch buffets and is a popular meeting place for Trinis as well as cruisers.

There are a lot of shoreside facilities here for the visiting yachtsman, though if you need serious work done on your boat, you have to go to Chaguaramas. The marina can arrange for somebody to clean your boat, wax the hull, and even scrub your bottom. They will also assist you in acquiring any sort of help that you may need. Just speak to Joe in the office, he's very knowledgeable and friendly, a real help to the cruising visitor at *TTYC*. And by the way, as you walk down the dock to the office, don't forget to say hello to Kaiso, the blue and gold Macaw in his huge cage by the office.

Within walking distance are several places to dine, pick up some groceries, ship a package, and get medical assistance. If you walk out to the Western Main Road past the guard shack (*TTYC* has EXCELLENT security), take a left and a hundred yards away is *Linda's La Cafe Francais*....what can I say? Fresh bread, croissants, baguettes, all sorts of delicious baked goodies, you can spend a ton here and put on just about that much weight as well. Linda also has tables if you care to sit down and relax while munching on a pain chocolate. Another few yards down the road and across the street are several facilities in a strip mall type of complex. These include a bank with an *ATM*, a hardware store, a nice *Hi-Lo Supermarket*, the *Glencoe Pharmacie* (*Western Union* with a package shipment service), and a medical clinic. You will also fond a nice Chinese Restaurant (daily lunch buffets with an extraordinary Wednesday night buffet), a couple of fast food take out places, and another French restaurant and bakery.

About a mile to the east of *TTYC*, is the three-story *Westmoorings Mall*, a great place to visit and shop. Here you will see several bookstores, a gym, a dentist's office, a good fabric shop, many clothing and shoe stores, a 1-hour photo lab, and a great food court. Next door is the new huge *Hi-Lo Supermarket* which just opened in September of 2001. There are two machines at the *ATM* inside the *Royal Bank* facing the road, which will allow you to withdraw cash in either TT or U.S. dollars. If you don't feel like walking here, just cross the road from *TTYC* and climb aboard a maxi-taxi. Jesse James will also pick you up here for his weekly shopping trips. Call Jesse's *Members Only* maxi-taxi service on VHF ch. 16. The Westmoorings area was once a swamp that was filled in during the 1940's. Just past the mall, on the north side of the road, is a hospital. A short distance past the mall on the same side of the road, is the huge *Peake's Hardware* store.

If you're staying at *TTYC* and have friends from back home visiting, there is a great little guesthouse not far from *TTYC*. *Tammy's Bed & Breakfast* is in Glencoe, the neighborhood across the Western Main Road about 1 block from *TTYC* (29 Strathavan Rd., Glencoe). Tammy offers daily and weekly rates, free transportation for your guests, and she even monitors VHF ch. 68. You can phone Tammy at 637-3707.

Port of Spain

Sprawled out between the Gulf of Paria and the mountain range to the north, Port of Spain, the capital of Trinidad since 1757, is the very heart of Trinidad, the cultural, economic, and social center of the island. The majestic twin *Central Bank* towers, that are landmarks along the waterfront also grace the back of TT dollar bills. At night the view is dazzling, twinkling lights dot the hills above the city from Carenage in the northwest to Arima in the east. Port of Spain is quite cosmopolitan, with over 1.2 million inhabitants living in a melange of different cultures spread about the surrounding suburbs.

There is one anchorage in Port of Spain, just off the St. Vincent Jetty. The wreck-strewn shallows just south of it offer a fair degree of protection in southeast winds and the holding is good in mud. The main problem here is theft. Be sure to lock your dingy up here at night. Many cruisers use this anchorage as a base for *Carnival*, it's convenient of course, but the security at Chaguaramas, lacking as it may be at times, is better than in Port of Spain. You'll feel far more vulnerable here, but don't let that dissuade you, taking good security measures, locking your dinghy and your hatches, will usually suffice. Don't leave anything on deck or in the cockpit that you don't want to lose. And a better idea would be not to leave the boat unattended at night, this means somebody's going to have to miss *J'Ouvert*.

Heading for Port of Spain from Chaguaramas or *TTYC*, you can parallel the shore, but you'll have to stay a good two miles out or more, the inshore waters are shoal and littered with wrecks that nobody has charted with any degree of accuracy. The waypoint I give is for the seaward end of Grier Channel, but you can just as easily pick up the channel between green buoys "3" and "7" if visibility is good and you don't mind a bit of shallow water, anywhere from 9'–15'.

As shown on Chart TRI-12, a GPS waypoint 10° 38.10' N, 61° 33.40 W, will place you approximately ¼ mile west/southwest of the entrance to Grier Channel, just outside the first buoys. When approaching the port remember that it is a commercial facility and give the large ships and tugs the right of way. Proceed down the channel towards King's Wharf and turn to starboard once past R "8". Work your way to the southeastern tip of the wharf where you'll see the St. Vincent Jetty off your bow. Anchor off the jetty in about 12'–30' of water. A lot of freighters and other commercial vessels anchor here, the holding is good, but it can be crowded with larger vessels at times. As you enter the Grier Channel, bear in mind that you might encounter a southeasterly current, an eddy of the northward flowing current in the Gulf of Paria. This eddy may be as strong as ½ knot on the flood and up to 1½ knots on the ebb.

Just south of the Grier Channel is the Sea Lots Channel, which is used primarily by commercial fishing vessels. The small harbor at the end of the channel offers good protection if needed, but it will be crowded if a major storm threatens (better to go to Puerto La Cruz or Laguna Grande in Venezuela). As you enter the harbour as shown on the chart, R "10" is missing, but the concrete piling remains. You can anchor in the southern portion of the bay, between the large ships that lie wrecked on the shore and the mangroves. Security is as important here as in Port of Spain.

There is a lot to see and do in Port of Spain, and I suggest that the best way to see it is to stay at *TTYC* or Chaguaramas and catch a maxi-taxi into town. So where do we begin? An entire guide could be written on Port of Spain itself and I can in no way show you everything here so I'll just touch on the highlights, anyway, exploring and discovery are some of the biggest joys of cruising, right? Go out and explore, keep you wallet in your front pocket gentleman, and ladies keep your money on you, leave nothing in your purse that you don't wish to lose. This is not a warning folks, think of it as precautions that you should take as you would in any large city, this is certainly not an indictment of the people of Port of Spain.

If you take a maxi-taxi downtown, you can get off anywhere you like or at the main station, *Citygate*, across from the *Port Authority* at Kings Wharf. This is also where you can take the ferry to Tobago if you'd like. If driving in a rental car, your best bet is to park in a pay-lot, there's one on the left just past the twin *Central Bank* towers. If you park on the streets, you can get towed away very quickly. Heading into Port of Spain you'll pass *Westmoorings Mall*, and just about a mile further on the road will split, you need to take the left hand branch, the Winston Road turnoff, that circles back under the right hand branch which goes straight into St. James. The left-hand road (Winston Road) takes you along the shoreline by the Stadium and into Port of Spain and the palm tree lined promenade in front of the *Port Authority*. If you continue on this road you will eventually come to the *Uriah Butler Highway* which is the road south to the *Caroni Swamp*, Chaguanas, and San Fernando.

If you decide to head into St. James, you'll enter the "city that never sleeps." There the street vendors are open 24 hours and people stroll the street all night. A lot of local men come here to meet local women and party all night long. St. James was originally a sugar plantation and the flavor today is East Indian. As the Western Main Road passes through here, you'll find the sidewalks wall to wall fast food establishments, bars, lottery houses, music stores, and numerous small stalls selling everything from East Indian foodstuffs to shoes, ice cream, colorful t-shirts, leather goods, and locally made crafts. Visitor should pay a visit to *Smokey and Bunty's*, the local bar named for the nicknames of the owners. To the east of St. James is Laventille, a poorer section of town, that is known for being the place where Spanish astronomer Don Cosmos Damien Churruca set up an observatory, the first in the New World.

The harbor at Port of Spain was dredged to handle deep draft ships in 1935. Prior to that the ships lay at anchor and passengers and cargo were ferried ashore. Directly across the street from the port is *Independence Square*, built on reclaimed swampland in 1816 by Baron Shack, who imported trees from Venezuela to line the road. Named *Independence Square* in 1962 when Trinidad and Tobago gained their independence, it was formerly called *Marine Square*, and during WW II, gained notoriety as the *Gaza Strip*. At this time dozens of night clubs lined Wrightson Road, complete with booze and strippers, and U.S. servicemen would party here all night long, even though nightly raids were common.

Nearby Frederick Streets is the heart of Port of Spain shopping. Many Trinis have their clothes hand made and buy their fabric here. Lining the streets in this area are dozens of fabric shops, as well as clothing and shoe shops, a lot of shoe shops. Sherry, owner of *Sherry's Laundry* at *Tardieu Marine* in Chaguaramas, is a good seamstress and can make a shirt, dress, shorts, or a pair of pants for you. Come here to buy our fabric and then take it to Sherry, you will not be dissatisfied. Just off Frederick St., by the Arthur Cipriani statue, is the *Drag Brothers Mall*, a dozen or so small leather shops where if you don't find what you want, they'll make it for you. A bit further east is the *Cathedral of the Immaculate Conception,* built in 1836 (started in 1820 and completed in 1836). At the corner of Frederick St. and Keate St. is the *National Museum and Art Gallery*. Built in 1892, the museum houses an extensive collection of exhibits as well as special section on *Carnival* and *Pan* Music

Port of Spain has its share of forts for you to visit. In Laventille, across from the Catholic Church, sits *Fort Chacon*, built by Spanish Governor Chacon in 1770. High above Laventille sits *Fort Picton*, another one of the oldest forts on the island. Named after British Governor Picton, it was built in 1797 when the British took over. *Fort George* has the best view from atop the hills above Port of Spain. *Fort George* was built by British Governor Sir Thomas Hislop in 1805 to further expand the protection of Port of Spain. The British were fearful that the Spanish would yet retaliate for the British takeover in 1797, or that the French whose fleet was nearby, might be planning their own invasion. Today you can still see the original cannon, dungeon, cannon balls and other items that the soldiers used. On South Quay, east of King's Wharf, is *Fort St. Andres,* a wooden fort built in 1787. Behind the large Victorian building on South Quay stands the old Port of Spain lighthouse, looks out of place inland in the middle of a traffic island. The lighthouse is the Trini version of the *Leaning Tower of Pisa* as it leans 5° due to the thundering traffic that passes by 24 hours a day.

Downtown° you'll find the *Queen's Park Savannah*, the heart of Port of Spain, the center of its culture, and the focus of *Carnival*. Once part of sugar estate owned by the Peschier family, the area was sold to the city in 1817 with the exception of the small family cemetery that still lies in the middle of the *Savannah* and which is still used by family members. Attempts were made to convert the area into a housing area in 1890, but vigorous opposition quashed those plans. But for decades after many more attempts were made to use parts of the *Savannah* for this reason or that, but the city planners would not give in.

Today Trinis flock to the park during all seasons. In February for *Carnival*, in the summer for kite-flying, and on weekends for family outings. The streets lining the Savannah are home to seven of the most beautiful architectural masterpieces on the island. You'll gaze in awe at what is known as the *Magnificent Seven*, seven buildings of Scottish, Moorish, Spanish, French, and Victorian roots.

Next to the Savannah are the *Botanical Gardens* and the *Emperor Valley Zoo*. The *Botanical Gardens* house the official residences of the President and the Prime Minister. The gardens were laid out in 1820 by Governor Woodford and David Lockhart, the first curator of the gardens. Governor Woods is buried in the small cemetery on the grounds (along with many former governors of the island), *God's Acre* as it's known. The collection of native and non-native trees is impressive, and in a grove of palm trees, an Australian wallaby is buried. The wallaby was a pet of the Prince of Wales that died while the Prince was on a trip to Trinidad.

The *Emperor Valley Zoo,* built in 1952, is probably the best zoo in the Caribbean. The birds, reptiles, fish, and mammals all live in habitats closely resembling their natural habitat. Just off the *Savannah* is an American dining institution, *TGI Friday's*.

South of Chaguaramas, just off the *Butler Highway,* is a popular spot for tourists, the *Caroni Swamp*. Here you can take guided tours to see the elusive scarlet ibis. These birds come in to nest in the evening hours so tours usually don't begin until 1500 or later. As you drive down the *Uriah Butler Highway* you'll soon see the exit for the *Caroni Bird Sanctuary*. Get off and the tour operations are right at the end of the exit to the south. *Nanan's Tours,* 645-1305, leaves at 1600, *Kalpoos,* 645-8452, leaves at 1500, and *James Madoo Tours,* 622-7356, who can also arrange fishing trips for you. Their boats have no motors, and you'd better bring a hat, sunglasses, and a good supply of bug spray. I got lucky one day as I was riding down the *Butler Highway* past the *Caroni Swamp*. I happened to look to the west over the swamp and saw two beautiful scarlet ibis casually flying along a quarter-mile off the highway.

South of the *Caroni Swamp* on the *Uriah Butler Highway* is Chaguanas, the third most important community on Trinidad, one of Trinidad's oldest settlements, a center of East Indian culture, and a shopper's delight. Chaguanas is also the location of

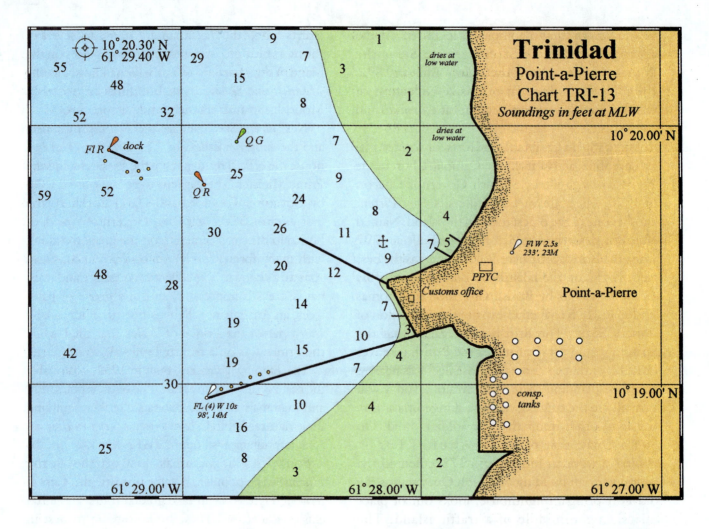

the *Lion House*, the former home of V.S. Naipaul, the Trini novelist who now lives in London. In his 1961 novel, *A House of Mr. Biswas*, Naipaul describes his early years growing up in the house.

The name is derived from the name of an Amerindian tribe that lived here at one time, the *Chaguanes*. The town prospered during the mid-1800's when thousands of East Indians arrived to work at the surrounding plantations. By the latter 19th century Chaguanas became the most important market towns in Trinidad. After the decline of the sugar industry, the inhabitants turned to other more white-collar professions creating the intelligentsia that spawned V.S. Naipaul. With the blossoming oil industry, Chaguanas became a center for southern Trinis who didn't wish to travel all the way to Port of Spain for shopping.

In town there are two large malls, as well as a *Price Smart* on the *Uriah Butler Highway*, but the place most visitor wish to see, and shop, is the market on the southern side of Main Road. Here you can stroll through acres of small stalls and sheds selling everything from fresh produce to crafts, clothing, jewelry, and shoes.

Just north of Chaguanas on the *Uriah Butler Highway*, you'll see a 36' tall statue of Swami Vivekananda, the Calcutta born 19th century force for Indian education. The *Uriah Butler Highway* was originally the *Princess Margaret Highway* when it opened in 1955. It was soon renamed for Uriah "Buzz" Butler, an oilfield worker who organized labor strikes in 1937.

About four miles south of Chaguanas on the Southern Main Road you'll find a row of pottery stalls. The earth in this area has a high clay content, not suitable for farming, but perfect for pottery. Every year, potters make thousands of small earthen pots (deyas) for the annual *Diwali* festival. But there is more than small clay pots to be found here, a complete range of pottery is available, and if you have something particular in mind, some of the potters will make it for you.

A bit further down the Southern Main Road you'll come to Friendship Hall, a fascinating old estate house with a turret, complex balconies, and wrought iron trimmings. Built in 1864 by Scotsman Hugh MacLeod, the house is still occupied by his family.

Point-a-Pierre

Heading south from Port of Spain, the only reasonable anchorage is at Point-a-Pierre, lying just south of Cangrejos Point and the heavy industrial complexes and marked channels at Point Lisas (TRI-1). If heading south you can parallel the shore, but stay off at least three miles as shoals stretch out a good distance from shore between Port of Spain and San Fernando, and wrecks litter the inshore areas. A good landmark is the oddly-shaped hill at San Fernando. Once a quarry, the hill is now protected.

Point-a-Pierre is home to a huge refinery, formerly a *Texaco* refinery, it was acquired by the Government of Trinidad and Tobago in 1984. During WW II, Point-a-Pierre was under heavy security because of its industrial areas. Make no doubt about it, Point-a-Pierre is still a heavy industrial area and your senses will pick that up. First, when approaching, you will see the smoke that is inherent in heavily industrialized areas, second, your nose will likely pick up the smells of industry, however the anchorage and the *Point-a-Pierre Yacht Club* (*PPYC*) are in a decent area and the *Point-a-Pierre Wildfowl Trust* should not be missed.

As shown on Chart TRI-13, a waypoint at 10° 20.30' N, 61° 29.40' W, will place you approximately 1 mile northwest of the anchorage area. Just to the south of this waypoint you'll see an offshore bunker that tankers use. Further south is a mile-long dock that stretches out from the point. From the waypoint, head in between the lit buoys as shown on the chart and work your way in north of the smaller dock to anchor off the *Yacht Club* docks in 10'–20' of water. *PPYC* has a dinghy dock, though no slips or fuel. The yacht club is primarily for oil industry employees and the bar is only open on weekends. *PPYC* is located on the grounds of the *Petrotrin Oil Refinery*, at the edge of the *Point-a-Pierre Wildfowl Trust*, the only nature reserve in the Caribbean maintained by the oil industry. Many species of duck and birdlife call the area home and there are breeding programs in place for the scarlet ibis.

Just north of Point-a-Pierre at Point Lisas, a migration takes place every year between December and June. Across from the industrial complexes lies a large swamp, and every year thousands of blue crabs make the dangerous trek across a busy road to lay their eggs in the sea. At this time the road is littered with crushed blue crabs.

San Fernando

A few miles south of Point-a-Pierre is the larger town of San Fernando, known as the "Capital of the South." *Sando*, as it is sometimes called, is second only in size to Port of Spain, the city is built on the hills on shore and life moves along here at a slower pace than in Port of Spain. The most notable landmark in San Fernando is the huge hill that dominates the area. The hill is prominent in Amerindian legends as the final resting place of *Haburi the Hero* and his mother who were fleeing from the *Frog Woman* in the Orinoco delta in Venezuela. They had reached the safety of *Ieri* (Trinidad), only to be caught and turned into *Anaparima*, the Amerindian name for the hill. Amerindians made pilgrimages to the site since many centuries before the birth of Christ up until the 1800's. At one time the hill was controlled by the landowners who owned the land at the base of the hill. The landowners discovered that the hill produced fine gravel and began to quarry the rock until stopped by the government. The hill was designated a National Park in 1980, and today it has been enhanced with plantings and benches and offers a scenic view of the city of San Fernando.

The first European visitor was Sir Walter Raleigh who was not impressed by the area and bypassed it. Capuchin monks established a mission here in 1642, but it wasn't until the latter 1700's when the area would flourish. In 1784, French plantation owners were granted lands in the surrounding areas

Church in Santa Cruz Trinidad.

and established huge estates. In 1786, the Spanish Governor, Jose Maria Chacon, renamed the settlement San Fernando de Naparima in honor of King Carlos III's new son (the surrounding areas are known as the *Naparimas*). By the time the British took over in 1797, San Fernando had over a thousand settlers, 20 mills, and 8 rum distilleries. By 1811, the population had tripled and in 1846 San Fernando was officially designated a town when British Governor Lord Harris improved the infrastructure of the town (a main promenade was named after him). The town became the hub for transshipments of goods for the southern part of Trinidad with a regular steamer to Port of Spain (the overland route took three days at this time). The population grew as a railroad was constructed in the 1880's and when sugar industry took a downturn in the 1920's, San Fernando turned to the oil industry to bolster its economy.

There is no comfortable anchorage in the area of San Fernando, the waters are shoal quite a distance off. The town dock is in disrepair as are several of the buildings onshore, also it is not in the best part of town. The *San Fernando Yacht Club*, is primarily for smaller powerboats, with depths of less than 5' at MLW. There is a bar on the premises and groceries and restaurants are nearby. The *SFYC* sells gas only and can help arrange for propane. The docks have power and water and the *SFYC* will do their best to accommodate a visiting boat, but can't promise anything.

The best way to visit San Fernando is by maxi-taxi from Port of Spain, or by car rental. The shopping, especially the fabrics, are priced better here than in Port of Spain. There area lots of small shops and street vendor's stalls. The streets are alive with people. The *Chancery Lane Market* at the end of High Street is a good stop for fresh produce and local crafts. A popular meeting spot in Sando is "the corner", the corner of High Street and Harris Promenade, Library Corner, with its non-functioning clock. Coffee Street dates back to the 1700's and is known as a hotbed of *Pan* music. The nearby panyard is decorated with colorful frescoes painted in 1995 by local artist Glen Steel. Known as the *Dancing Walls*, the painting trace the history

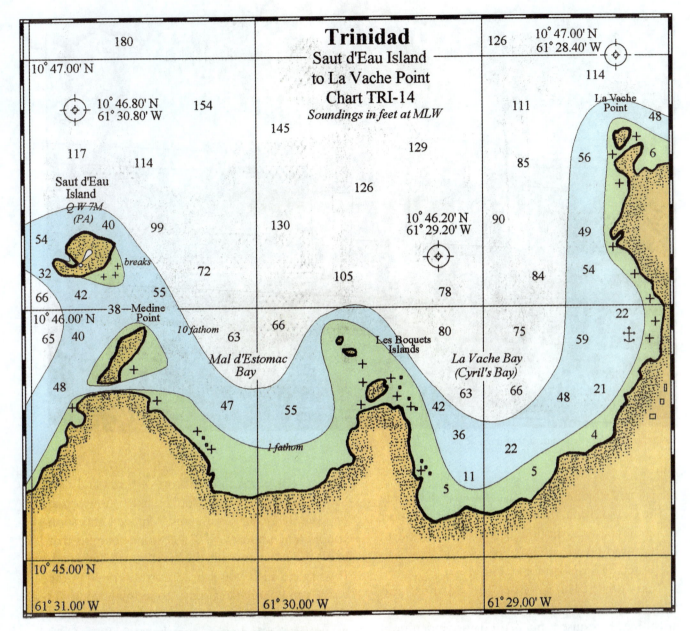

of *Pan* over the last half-century. Just outside of town is a huge three-story mall called *Gulf City*, with its huge *Hi-Lo* supermarket.

On the highway outside San Fernando, at the Claxton Bay turn-off, is a statue of a headless woman. Legend has it that the statue was erected by a local plantation overseer whose daughter had been having an affair with a laborer on his estate. The father, in an effort to keep his daughter away from the man, tried to lock his daughter in their home while he placed a snake at the location where she was to meet her lover in order to scare the young man away. The girl escaped and fled to meet her boyfriend where the snake ended her life. There have been a high number of accidents in the area that have been contributed to drivers seeing the ghost of the young girl who suddenly appears in front of their cars.

THE NORTHERN COAST

The northern coast of Trinidad is thick with forest, mountains, and sleepy fishing villages. Lying just a few miles inland, Mt. El Tucuche, the second highest peak in Trinidad, is easily seen from offshore. IN the 1800's cocoa was a huge source of income for Trinidadians and many cocoa plantations sprang up in the valleys along the northern coast. Even though

Lavache Bay, North Trinidad scenic view.

a small trail stretched from Blanchisseuse all the way to the Gulf of Paria, the principal mode of transport along the coast was the pirogue, the sturdy, wooden, high-bowed boat that ferried people and freight in the waters of Trinidad for centuries.

Just northeast of Boca de Monos and Chaguaramas lies Macqueripe Bay, not a good anchorage for cruisers, but in the days of indentured labor, ships ferrying the laborers to Trinidad would anchor here. Soon, a medical officer and other officials would board the ships before proceeding to the quarantine stations at Nelson Island in the Five Islands area. The U.S. acquired the land around the bay in the Lend-Lease arrangement with Great Britain. Near Macqueripe Bay stands a great navigational landmark shown as "structure" on some charts. It's actually the remains of an old OMEGA station that is used as a beacon for local navigators. Today Macqueripe Bay is a popular beach hang-out that was a favorite of Errol Flynn in years past.

If you wish to access this coast by land, go to *Queen's Park Savannah* in Port of Spain and take Saddle Road northward. You'll make your way past *St. Andrew's Golf Course* and Maravel, and soon you'll come upon two 10' tall stone columns that mark the junction with the Northern Main Road. If you take a left you'll head northward along the coast, and if you take a right, continuing along the Saddle Road, you'll work your way through a narrow mountain pass and arrive at the beautiful Santa Cruz Valley. Keeping on the Saddle Road you'll pass Cantaro and wind up in San Juan, a suburb of Port of Spain. However, if you continue up the Northern Main Road you will pass through some of the most breathtaking scenery on the island of Trinidad.

The Northern Main Road is one of the most scenic roads in the entire Caribbean. At certain spots on the road you'll see a bamboo pipe jutting out of the rock or underbrush. Stop here to sample some cool, fresh, spring water, or bring a few empty jerry-jugs to take some back with you. The road itself was built by the U.S. Army as an expression of gratitude by the military for use of the Chaguaramas peninsula. The American military occupation of this

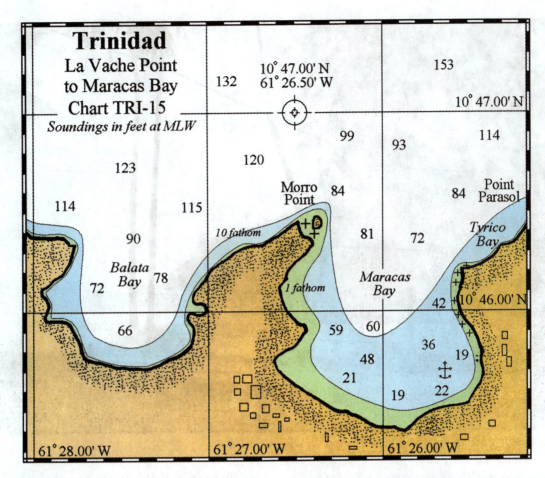

area effectively closed off the beaches at Macqueripe and the folks from Carenage and Port of Spain had to go further, to Maracas Beach, for the weekend retreat. This is why the road is sometimes called the American Road. The road brings you to the La Vache Bay area in a short while, and since you can also access the bay by boat, we'll discuss that now.

La Vache Bay

If approaching from the Bocas, keep at least ½ mile offshore to make your way to a GPS waypoint at 10° 46.80' N, 61° 30.80' W, which will place you ½ mile north of Saut d'Eau Island as shown on Chart TRI-14. If approaching from Grenada or Tobago, you can also make your way to this waypoint. Vessels can also pass between Saut d'Eau Island and the mainland, but I won't give you a waypoint for this, you will have to pilot your way through by eye, but keep an eye out for the shoals south of Saut d'Eau Island. There is a little know channel between the island called Medine Point and the mainland where deep water reaches close to shore. This is not a recommended route, but just a bit of local knowledge for you. Another tidbit is that the Saut d'Eau area is a good spot for kingfish.

From the waypoint north of Saut d'Eau head generally southeast toward a waypoint at 10° 46.20' N, 61° 29.20' W, which places you ½ mile northwest of the anchorage in La Vache Bay sometimes called Cyril's Bay. Give Les Boquets Islands a wide berth. Mal d'Estomac is not a good choice for anchoring, it is deeper than La Vache Bay and does not offer the protection that La Vache Bay does and its bottom is rocky. Anchor about halfway down the eastern side of the bay off the northernmost of two small beaches.

Saut d'Eau Island is a breeding area for brown pelicans and other seabirds. La Vache Bay is known for its fresh water spring and Venezuelan fishing boats having been coming here for years to fill up their tanks.

Ashore is the well-known *Timberline Resort* complete with a restaurant with a remarkable view of the northern coast of Trinidad. It seems that

TRINIDAD • 63

The lovely beach at Maracas Bay, northern shore of Trinidad.

there's no end to the scenic views on this stretch of coast. At the southern end of the anchorage you'll find a stone house, the home of Frank McCume, a guide to the best diving, waterfalls, and caves in the area. You'll be welcomed by Frank's menagerie of dogs, ducks, and geese, and Frank can show you how to get to a 10' waterfall that he built to supply his drinking water. Please don't ask to swim there.

On the road heading north out of La Vache Bay, stop at the *Hot Bamboo Hut* for a cold drink and to view the toucans. Between 1600 and 1800, you can often get the owner to call the flock of toucans that live in the forest above the bar. Proceeding onwards you'll come to one of the most scenic spots on the coast, the La Vache Lookout. Here you'll find a large parking lot and lookout point with vendors selling various crafts and candies from glass jugs called *safes*. On the weekends you'll probably be serenaded by a busker, one who improvises *calypso* for money. He'll expect a few dollars from you if he makes you laugh, and chances are, he will make you laugh. Heading down from the lookout point you'll approach the most popular stop on the northern coast, Maracas Bay.

Maracas Bay

One of the most popular stops along the northern coast of Trinidad is Maracas Bay, a good spot to overnight before heading on to Tobago. Weekends, especially Sundays, finds the beach packed with Trinis swimming and dining on the local favorite, *Shark n' Bake*, a sweet pastry dough, similar to a doughnut, filled with shark and with a huge choice of condiments to adorn it. If you don't like shark, some of the food stalls will serve you kingfish instead. *Richard's* and *Natalie's* serve up some of the best *Shark n' Bake* and are located in the car park. Ash Wednesday is also packed as *Carnival* merry-makers come here to relax after the energy draining *Carnival*. The *Bay View Restaurant*, just west of the beach area, has a great view and good food, though not to match *Natalie's*. At the eastern end of the beach is *Uncle Sam's*, THE spot for loud music and cold drinks. At the western end of the beach is the town of Maracas where most of the residents can claim mixed Spanish and Amerindian descent.

If approaching from La Vache Bay, pass well to seaward of La Vache Point and make your way to a waypoint at 10° 47.00' N, 61° 26.50' W, will place you approximately 1 mile northwest of Maracas Bay as shown on Chart TRI-15. Head in toward the beach and anchor in the southeastern corner to get out of any surge that may work its way in. Don't even try to anchor in Balata Bay as it is deeper, has more surge, and has a rocky bottom.

Just outside Maracas is the Magnetic Road between La Vache Bay and Maracas Bay. If approaching Maracas Bay from La Vache Bay, stop just before the North Coast Road begins its descent to Maracas Bay. Stop where the cliffs to the right recede and the road appears to begin a slight incline. Keeping your foot on the brakes, put the car in neutral. Taking your foot off the brake you would think that the car would roll backward down the incline, instead the car begins to inch slowly forward, apparently defying gravity. Nobody knows for sure what causes this, most think it's just an optical illusion, but it's something to try. I am from the Atlanta, Georgia area, and just outside Atlanta, in Cumming, Georgia, we have a similar attraction, Booger Road, but, that's another tale for another guide.

Las Cuevas Bay

The next bay is called Las Cuevas Bay, Spanish for *caves*, where the Curagate River flows into the bay creating sandy hollows in the banks. As shown on Chart TRI-16, a GPS waypoint at 10° 47.30' N, 61° 24.00' W, will place you approximately ½ nautical mile NW of Las Cuevas Bay. If approaching from Maracas Bay, give Point Parasol a bit of a berth, you can stay ¼ mile off and be safe of dangers here. As you enter Las Cuevas Bay, head in towards the fishing fleet anchoring just outside them in 15'-30' of water. Bear in mind that a bit of swell works its way in here in normal conditions, and during periods of northerly swells the anchorage is untenable.

There are many caves on the western shore of the bay and actually in the seabed as well. The bottom is rocky and the holding ranges from poor to good here, and then there's the vicious sandfly population. Ashore however, there is a very nice public beach with shower facilities and *McLean's Bar* at the car park. The *Las Cuevas Rec Club* is a highly informal place to get a cold drink. East of *Las Cuevas Beach* is *Thousand Steps Beach*, named after the numerous concrete steps leading down the cliff to the sand below. The path leading to the beach begins about ¼ mile east of Las Cuevas Bay.

Across the Northern Main Road from Las Cuevas is a small road named Rincon Trace that will lead you to Rincon Falls, after a 2½ uphill hike of course. You'll need a guide for this one, call Laurence Pierre at 632-4204, and ask Laurence to take you to *Angel Falls* as well.

Inland from Las Cuevas you'll find Mount El Tucuche, and south of this peak the 300' high Maracas Waterfall. Although one could hike to the falls from Maracas Bay, a difficult 8-hour hike at best, the easiest way to view the falls starts with a rental car. Drive east on the Eastern Main Road from Port of Spain to the town of St. Joseph, the first capital of Trinidad, and go north on the Maracas Royal Road until you come to Waterfall Road, about 8km from the Eastern Main Road. A few minutes down this road you'll come to your guide's house, Trevor Raymond. It's best to take a guide through here, and Trevor will usually come out to meet any car that approaches. After you park you'll take a wide rocky path for about 15 minutes until you arrive at a smaller trail to the right. This takes you to the first cascade, three tiers of small falls with very cold pools at the bottom suitable for taking a dip. The main cascade is still another 20-30 minutes away. As you approach you'll begin to see signs that say "No Candles" and won't have a clue as to what they mean until you near the falls and see numerous old candles and pools of wax on the surrounding rocks and colorful prayer flags blowing in the breeze. The falls are a special place for Hindus, Baptists, and others who come here for private rituals that only lend an eerie air to the beautiful falls. The falls are almost 300' and Trevor can lead you the top and the *Three Pools*, three small pools where Trevor has built a grill and camping spot.

Chupara Point

Proceeding along the northern coast the only other protection is in the lee of Chupara Point in La Fillete Bay (the point is marked by a light), but it is often rough there as well. This is a good spot to anchor overnight before continuing on to Tobago. As shown on Chart TRI-16, a GPS waypoint at 10° 49.00' N, 61° 23.85' W, will place you approximately ½ mile northwest of the rocks that are awash west of Chupara Point (when approaching from either direction, give this area a wide berth). If approaching from Tobago, head well west of Chupara Point before turning south to enter the anchorage in La Fillete Bay. If approaching from Las Cuevas, round Abercromby Point and its offlying rock, and head for La Fillete Bay staying ½ mile offshore to avoid submerged rocks just inshore. You can anchor in Fillete Bay just west of the white house and the older estate house that sits behind it (as shown on the chart). Try to anchor in as close to shore as your draft allows, this anchorage does get some swell at times, and during periods of northerly swells is untenable. Ashore you'll find a small beach with a path that leads up to the road. Another path, leading off to the north just before the road, leads you to Chupara Point Light.

As the northern road proceeds along the northern coast from Las Cuevas, the road twists and turns, rising and descending, hardly wide enough for two vehicles at times with the narrow wooden bridges over the Yarra River being only wide enough for one car. Just offshore is a rock that bears the painted slogan "Yarradise Bay." Inland you have an excellent view of Mt. El Tucuche, Trinidad's second highest mountain. Further east is another offshore rock labeled "Hollyweed," presumably after the baled product that is said to move through this area.

From the Yarra River, the next settlement to the east is Blanchisseuse, the last before the road fades out and you must turn south towards the *Asa Wright Nature Center* on the Arima-Blanchisseuse Road. Blanchisseuse is home to some 3,000 people and the homes indicate that this is not a sleepy fishing village, this is a favorite holiday spot with lots of accommodations. The town is actually made up of two communities, Lower Blanchisseuse lies to the west with several small homes, a few bars, a fisherman's co-op, a post office, and a church. To the east you'll find Upper Blanchisseuse, the main residential settlement and home to the police station and several stores such as *Fattah's Foods*, *Lloyd's Leather Crafts*, and the *Cocos Hut Restaurant*. Opposite the *Surf's Country Inn* are some concrete steps leading down to a beach that's popular with surfers. It's called, of course, *Surfer's Beach*, but its real name is *L'Anse Martin*.

You cannot proceed eastward from Blanchisseuse by car, but the trek to and from Paria Bay and its inland waterfall is a popular hike. The hardiest of trekkers continue on toward Matelot. Past Matelot is Toco, a picturesque fishing village at the northeastern tip of Trinidad. Isolated for so many years, it was finally connected to Port of Spain and other ports on Trinidad by steamer in the days of British rule.

Heading south of Blanchisseuse on the Arima-Blanchisseuse Road is a trip you won't forget. You'll begin a marvelous drive down a narrow, pot-holed, twisting, turning road with so many switchbacks that they'll soon begin to all look alike. This is one of the most stunning roads in the Caribbean. Make sure you have plenty of gas for the trip, as the next gas stop won't be until you reach Arima.

The tropical forest infringes upon the road so completely that at times you might wonder if you are indeed on the right road. You may feel you need to turn your lights on because the canopy is so heavy. The road at times will look as if within a week's time, the huge grasses and stands of bamboo will completely reclaim the road. Keep your window down to listen for car horns at curves, and honk yours as you approach every bend to warn oncoming vehicles. Just before the 20¼ marker you'll find a small group of houses with a trail leading past them to Avocat Falls. A ten minute hike will take you to a river where you can turn left and follow the bank for twenty minutes until you reach a junction with another stream. Wade across the stream and climb the steep bank and voilá, 36' Avocat Falls. Take a well-deserved dip in the pool at the base.

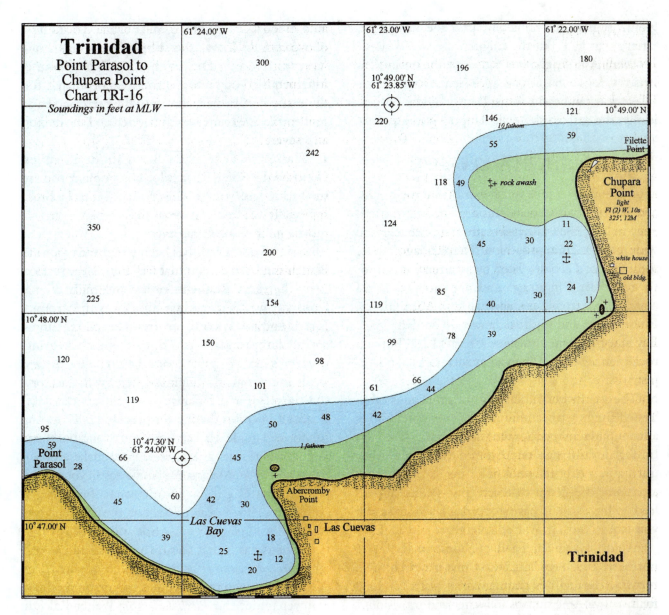

Proceeding down the road to Arima you'll come to Morne la Croix, where most of the folks still speak French Creole as well as Trini English. All along this road you'll have sweeping views of mountains and valleys, absolutely breathtaking, a don't miss drive. Past Brasso Seco you'll soon come to the *Asa Wright Nature Center*, a nature-lover's paradise. The center was originally a coffee and cocoa plantation. In 1947, the land was purchased by Dr. Newcome Wright. With his wife Asa, both naturalists and bird-watchers, soon accommodated visiting researchers at the neighboring *New York Zoological Society's Simla Tropical Research Station*. When Dr. Wright died, Asa sold the land on the condition it be used as a conservation area and a non-profit Trust was created in 1967 to maintain the Wright's land as a nature center. *Simla* closed in 1970 and donated their land to the *Asa Wright Center*, which today hosts numerous researchers and tourists on their beautiful grounds.

The heart of the center is the 90 year-old great house with its polished mahogany floors and balcony that overlooks the surrounding valleys. The restaurant serves a daily buffet, sandwiches, and of course, cold drinks.

Jesse James's *Members Only* maxi-taxi service makes regular trips to the center, call Jesse on VHF ch. 68 for more information. *Trump Tours* sometimes makes a run here as well. There is a lovely lodge at the center and you will really enjoy your visit here, but bring bug spray, the mosquitoes aren't that bad, but the chiggers are world class.

From Asa Wright the rainforest wanes and the road widens a bit as you approach Arima. From there you can head back to Port of Spain, or head down the eastern shore via Sangre Grande.

THE SOUTHERN AND EASTERN COASTS

While the southern and eastern coasts can in no way be described as cruising grounds, there are no secure anchorages to speak of, the area is still quite beautiful and is best visited by an arranged tour or by rental car. I'm going to assume that you have a rental car, and will describe what you can find on these coasts and in the interior of Trinidad. Many of these places are shown on Chart TRI-1, but you can pick up a road-map at most marinas and car rentals.

The southwestern peninsula of Trinidad is often called the most beautiful part of the island and is sometimes referred to as the "deep south." The land is fertile and has been home to many sugar plantations over the years. The area also lays claim to being the first area where Europeans landed. Columbus is said to have stopped at Icacos to search for water and Sir Walter Raleigh is said to have caulked his ships at La Brea (home of the *Pitch Lake*) in 1595. Raleigh, who came in search of *El Dorado*, the mythical city of gold, supposedly traded with native Amerindians for water and provisions.

Five miles south of San Fernando on the Southern Main Road you'll come to the *Oropuche Lagoon*, a huge mangrove swamp alongside the road. There are no tours here and the government plans to keep it that way, maintaining the area as undisturbed by man as possible. However the swamp is threatened by old oil pumps that are all over the southern Trinidad area, over 1600, that were left to rust away and which often leak oil into the surrounding waters.

As the Southern Main Road crosses the Oropuche River, there is a crematorium on your right, the *Shore of Peace*. There are piles of lumber and logs stacked up for the next cremation when family members place their loved one atop the pyre and send them into eternity. The pyre areas are numbered and have a nice view of the Gulf of Paria. The nearby Godineau River was the scene of a famous Trini murder. Here, a Dr. Singh, killed his wife and dumped her body into the river. Unfortunately for him, the tide turned and brought the body back upstream. The crime was discovered and the doctor arrested.

The *Pitch Lake* at La Brea, about 12 miles southwest of San Fernando, is a popular tourist destination. As you get closer and closer to La Brea, especially the last couple of miles or so, you will notice pitch showing up everywhere, it will appear that everybody's yard has been paved with asphalt. This is merely the pitch that has risen to the surface over the years. Residents of the area must keep a constant watch over their abodes as the ground slowly undulates over the years and can cause shifting of building foundations. The lake itself is still being used as source of pitch (some of the finest quality asphalt in the world originates here) with a factory on the shore and a railway of small cars that take loads of pitch up the hill for processing. There are uniformed guides that can give you a tour, but there are also unofficial guides seeking to make a dollar or two off you. Make sure that you avail yourself of a legitimate guide. Don't wear high heels (obviously) if you plan to walk on the lake (you can walk on it in places, your guide will explain).

Legend has it that Carib Indians killed and ate the *Sacred Humming Bird*, which angered the *Great Spirit* who punished them by trapping them forever under the *Pitch Lake*. Sir Walter Raleigh stopped here in 1595 to apply pitch to his ships, but the lake was not used commercially until the time of the American Civil War in the 1860's. At this time the British began to remove pitch and continue to do so for a century until 1978 when Trinidad took over the operation.

Continuing on towards the southwestern tip at Icacos you will pass huge teak plantations which soon change to coconut palms as you approach the point. Cedros is the name of the area, not a settlement, and derived its name from the huge cedar trees that flourished here in the early 18th century, though none survive to present times. The Spanish influence is heavy in this area, Spanish being the primary tongue here almost until the beginning of the 20th century. Besides the cedars, Cedros was known far and wide on the island for its rum, the town once boasted seven distilleries. The area can claim almost the same number of lovely, and usually deserted, beaches.

The *Boca del Serpiente*, the *Serpent's Mouth*, is the southern gateway to the Gulf of Paria at the extreme southwestern end of Trinidad. The *boca* was named by Columbus and has a strong current running through it although the Gulf of Paria is relatively calm itself. The point at Icacos lies only a few miles from Venezuela and is a popular spot for modern-day smugglers bringing drugs into the island.

Well inland from Icacos lies Siparia, known for its feast of *La Divina Pastora*, the *Divine Shepherdess*. On the second Sunday after Easter, locals carry the statue of the Black Virgin through the streets while people, dressed in their best clothes, make offerings and make merry all day and most of the night. The statue, which has had many miracles attributed to it, serves dual religious duty. Some locals say that the statue was once the prow of a ship that was wrecked on Quinam Bay. Others claim the statue was brought to Siparia from Venezuela by a priest whose life it had saved while fleeing from an Amerindian revolt. In the 1890's, Hindu indentured servants decided that the statue was the goddess *Kali*, the destroyer of sorrow, and they renamed the statue *Soparee Kay Mai*. If the statue answers their prayers, Hindu women offer it locks of hair cut from their children's first haircut. The Catholic Church tried to dissuade the fervent Hindus in 1920, but to no avail as many still worship the statue.

The southern shore is dotted with small fishing villages and few amenities. The south-central region of Trinidad consists of rolling hills that stretch from Princes Town in the north, to Icacos in the southwest, and Mayaro in the east. Oil wells dot the landscape, as well as the waters offshore (if you're planning to transit this area, get a good government chart of the area and keep your eyes open-the wells are well lit, but there are a lot of them). Road maps can be inaccurate here, the road you're looking for will likely be unmarked, and sometimes little more than a dirt path.

Heading east from San Fernando your first stop will be Princes Town, and it will be a stop, especially on the weekend when crowds throng through the street shopping and liming. I've driven through here before and have sat for over 30 minutes on the one-mile stretch through downtown. Just outside of town you will pass several small stalls offering "Fresh Goat." The goats tied up outside the stalls will testify that goat doesn't come any fresher.

Princes Town was originally a mission named Savanna Grande, when in 1880 Prince Albert and Prince George (who was later to become King), visited the mission to plant two *poui* trees at the old Anglican Church. The town was renamed Princes Town in their honor.

On the outside of Princes Town are the small communities of First, Third, Fourth, and Fifth Company, named after companies of black American soldiers. These former slaves fought for the British in exchange for land and were granted parcels in Trinidad. You'll notice that there is no Second Company, this unit was lost at sea on its way to Trinidad.

Heading east from Princes Town you pass the Devil's Woodyard with its mud volcanoes. These "volcanoes" are mud mounds about 3' tall that spew gray, sulfuric mud that is supposed to be good for the skin. These volcanoes can be found all over Trinidad, *TIDCO* even marks them on some of their tourist publications. They can be dangerous as they have a tendency to explode every few years. A recent explosion in Piparo destroyed a road in 1997. The Amerindians believed the volcanoes were links between this world and the world below and that the explosions were blamed on the Devil.

Moruga celebrates the fact that Columbus anchored here in 1498, but locally, the area is known more for Obeah. Papa Neiza was an African herbal doctor who was immortalized in *Calypso* songs. Today locals will tell tales of the Obeah woman Madame Cornstick, a very powerful woman, who still lives there, but is rarely seen. They'll speak in hushed tones of her, obviously in awe and in fear of her powers.

Rio Claro is the hub of southeastern Trinidad, both commercially and socially. Southeast of Rio Claro is Guayaguayare, a popular vacation spot for Trinis. Gazing out to sea there are several oil rigs on the horizon, while the shoreline is studded with oil tanks. Oil was first discovered here in 1819, but recent years brought a wave of fortune to local residents literally on the tide. A smuggler's boat was being chased by the Coast Guard offshore and dumped their load of cocaine overboard. The majority of the drug parcels washed up on the beach where happy locals gathered the packages before the authorities arrived. A vessel can anchor in the lee of the point, but be advised that there is a large shoal that works its way south of the point a good distance. The waters of the southern coast are thick with oil wells so use caution if you transit this area. Also be aware of the westerly current through here, 3–5 knots most of the time, but local mariners have told me they've seen the current as strong as 7 knots.

Aside the Rio Claro-Guayaguayare Road is the *Trinity Hills Wildlife Sanctuary*. The 65-square kilometer evergreen forest houses a watershed vital to Trinidad's water supply. The area was declared a reserve in 1900, and designated a wildlife sanctuary in 1934.

Starting at Guayaguayare, the eastern shoreline of Trinidad is one of the most beautiful areas of the island. North of Guayaguayare lies the town of Mayaro. Once home to a vast coconut plantation, Mayaro became well-known from 1914 to 1965 when the railroad was closed down. The tourism industry had a brief resurgence in the 1970's only to die again in the mid-1980's. Mayaro is comprised of two smaller communities, Pierreville and Plaisance. Pierreville is the business center of town while Plaisance is the seaside resort area. Here you'll find a nice fresh seafood shop right on the highway heading north.

Heading north from Mayaro, you will enter a gorgeous area called the *Cocal*, an uninterrupted coconut plantation stretching northward as far as Manzanilla. Here you'll drive through mile after mile of graceful, leaning coconut palms and the occasional royal palm. These trees, not in commercial use today, are said to be the descendants of coconuts washed ashore from a ship that foundered in a hurricane. The long windward beach, backed by miles of palm trees, is a popular spot with locals on weekends and holidays. You'll sometimes see huge leatherback turtles laying their eggs on the beaches here in early summer. There are many tours that will take you to the eastern beaches from Chaguaramas, try *Jesse James' "Members Only" Maxi-Taxi* or *Trump Tours* at *Crews Inn* for more information, both monitor VHF ch. 68 in Chaguaramas.

Heading north from Mayaro (on the coast road, you pass straight through the middle of the *Cocal* and the edge of the *Narvia Swamp*. There you'll find a lovely river whic can be explored by kayak. The swamp is home to 58 species of mammal including the maniteel, a cousin to the Florida manatee. The swamp is also home to large water snakes (anacondas from Venezuela), caimans, various parrots, ducks, howler monkeys, and many species of fish and birdlife (171 species of birds). On the down side, it is also home to 92 different species of mosquito. It's been said that large crocodiles have even turned up here after crossing the Gulf of Paria after being washed down the Orinoco in a flood. In the middle of the swamp is an island called the *Bush Bush Sanctuary*. Bordered by palm trees and covered in hardwoods and silk cotton trees, the island is not easy to get to and is unexploited by tour guides.

At the northern end of the *Cocal* is Manzanilla, actually Upper and Lower Manzanilla. On the eastern coast you'll find the Brigand Hill Lighthouse, built in 1958. You can't climb to the top, but you can scale the iron stairs on the outside of the lighthouse for a good view of the eastern coast including the *Cocal*, the *Nariva Swamp*, and the mountains to the north. From Manzanilla you can head to Sangre Grande on your way back to Port of Spain or Chaguaramas. A bit further west is Arima which has a special place in the culture of Trinidad.

Arima is home to the descendants of the original Carib Indians who occupied Trinidad when Columbus arrived. The local descendants prefer to be known as the *Kalina Nation*, saying that the term *Carib* is a European corruption of their name. The *Santa Rosa Carib Community Association* was formed in 1974 to preserve the interests of the shrinking tribe. Their office on Paul Mitchell Street sells traditional handicrafts and offers information about the tribe whose intermarriages are slowly eroding the physical attributes of these people.

Tobago

Unlike her neighbor, Trinidad, with its plethora of marine services, Tobago lies at the other end of the spectrum. Tobago has no marine services to even come close to what Trinidad offers, there are no marinas, nowhere to haul out, nowhere to get fuel save by jerry-jugging it, but this island offers quality cruising grounds and excellent diving and snorkeling opportunities. Not only that, the island has only the lightest touches of the tourism industry upon it. Where Trinidad is getting more and more cosmopolitan, Tobago remains laid back, the place to be on Ash Wednesday after giving your all during *Carnival*.

Tobago is approximately 21 miles long and about 7 miles wide at its widest, Tobago has a wide low-lying coastal plain along the southwestern shore rising to a central ridge of volcanic hills reaching almost 1900' in height. The central ridge of rain forest was set aside as a nature preserve in the 1780's making it the oldest such preserve in the New World. The rain forest was protected to maintain the purity of the water flowing through the network of streams, rivers, and waterfalls that lead from the mountains to the sea. It is said that water nymphs inhabit the cool mountain pools.

The Spaniards named the island after the y-shaped pipe that the native Amerindians used for smoking *kohiba*. The pipe, called *tobacco*, was inserted into the nostrils and the smoke inhaled until the smoker fell into a stupor. The Spaniards picked up this habit, but did not inhale to the point of intoxication, much like an American ex-president. Tobago is often said to be the model for the island in Robinson Crusoe, in fact, there is a cave on the southwestern tip of Tobago called Crusoe's Cave.

Vessels headed to Tobago from the north, from Grenada or Carriacou, must deal with the fluky northwest set of the *Guyana Current* that flows between Tobago and Grenada. Here you'll find the current pushing you westward at 2 knots at times, at other times you would have to look hard to find any current at all. Although cruisers often head for Tobago from the southern coast of Grenada, Prickly Bay or Hog Island, it is not recommended unless you have a good engine or simply like tacking. A better idea would be to head northward to Carriacou and then sail to Tobago from the northeastern tip of Carriacou or Petite St. Vincent. Another option is to sail to Tobago from Barbados to lay the island on one tack. Of course, those of us that don't like to go to weather might suggest that you head to the Azores and then down to the

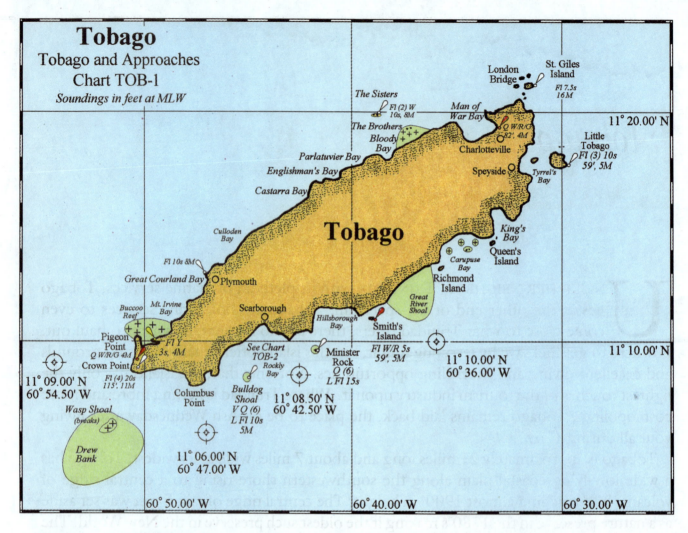

Canaries and back across the Atlantic to avoid headwinds. The choice is yours.

Vessels heading to Tobago from Trinidad have no other choice than to go against wind and current. Most cruisers make this trip in small hops, leaving from Scotland Bay and making Maracas Bay the first day by staying close inshore. Leaving Maracas Bay around midnight and hugging the coast at least 1½ miles off until between Chupara Point and Galera Point (see Chart TRI-1, both have lights), then changing course to account for the current and steering for the waypoint off Scarborough. The further east you go along the northern coast of Trinidad, the less you'll have to deal with the current between Tobago and Trinidad. I suggest going east as least as far as Grande Riviere.

When plotting your course from Trinidad to Scarborough, that you must deal with a current that will be flowing westward at 2 knots and more at times (Remember your high school geometry?). If you have crossed the Gulf Stream off Florida on your voyage to the Caribbean, you'll be familiar with the math involved and the same principle applies here. The only difference is that the body of water that you are crossing, the Galleon Passage, is only about 20 miles wide instead of 50 and Tobago is easily seen in good visibility. Try to time your passage so that you will arrive in Scarborough before the trades pick up in the morning, usually by 0800–0900.

Let's begin our tour of Tobago at Scarborough and work our way clockwise around the island, which is the best way for a vessel to circumnavigate the island. The northern coast in most conditions is a bit out of the current and the roughest part is often at the northeastern tip around the St. Giles Islands. Bear in mind that you won't want to be anchored anywhere along the northern coast during the winter

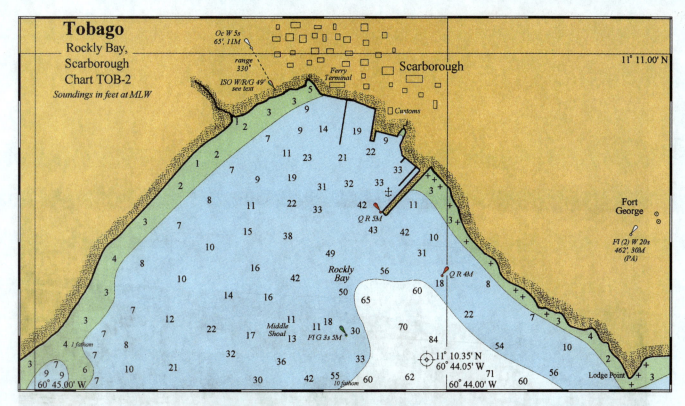

months when the northerly swells begin to roll in. At this time Scarborough or King's Bay are the best anchorages. Conversely, when a southeast wind is blowing Scarborough gets a bit rolly.

ROCKLY BAY, SCARBOROUGH

Vessels heading for Scarborough from the north, from Grenada or Carriacou, can head for a waypoint at 11° 09.00' N, 60° 54.50' W (as shown on Chart TOB-1), which will place you approximately 3 miles west of Crown Point and 3 miles northwest of Wasp Shoal. From this position pass between Wasp Shoal and the southwestern tip of Tobago and if you'd like, you can head straight for a waypoint at 11° 06.00' N, 60° 47.00' W which places you approximately 2 miles south of Columbus Point (bear in mind that once through the cut between Wasp Shoal and Crown Point, you will again be battling a westward setting current all the way to Scarborough). From this position, you can make your turn towards Rockly Bay and Scarborough giving Bulldog Shoal a wide berth to arrive at a waypoint 11° 08.50' N, 60° 43.00' W, which will place you approximately 2 miles southeast of the harbor in Rockly Bay and well clear of Bulldog Shoal. From this waypoint you can head for a waypoint a 11° 10.35' N, 60° 44.05' W, which places you just outside the lit buoys that mark the entrance channel to the harbor at Scarborough as shown on Chart TOB-2. As you enter the harbor you might notice an eastward flowing current, actually an eddy of the westward setting current that flows between Trinidad and Tobago. Pass between the buoys and round the tip of the jetty to starboard to anchor well out of the channel to the ferry dock as the ferry uses it daily arriving around 1900–2000. Be sure to show an anchor light here. Vessels heading from Scarborough to Crown Point and onward can follow the above directions and waypoints in reverse.

Home to 18,000 of the island's 40,000+ people, Scarborough retains a certain rustic charm much unlike her sister city of Port of Spain, Trinidad. Scarborough became the capital of Tobago in 1779. It is divided into two sections, Upper and Lower Scarborough, the latter located around the dock area, a port since the Dutch constructed a fort and dock here in 1654, and named the area Lampsinburgh. At the same time Latvians were setting up across the island at Plymouth. In 1658 the Dutch captured Plymouth and in 1666, an

The anchorage at Scarborough, Tobago.

English fleet, in retaliation, destroyed Lampsinburgh. But the English failed to maintain a presence and the Dutch returned a few years later and rebuilt the town as well as constructing a fort for its defense. The French attacked the settlement in 1677 and a French cannonball hit the ammunition dump which destroyed the fort and killed 250 Dutch settlers and soldiers. Nothing is left of the fort today but it is remembered by the name, Dutch Fort Road. The British regained control of Tobago in 1762 and named the settlement Scarborough. When the French took over again in 1781, Scarborough became Port Louis, while Fort King George became Fort Castries. The town bounced back and forth like a tennis ball until the British took control in 1814 and it remained under British rule until Trinidad and Tobago became one nation in 1976. Rockly Bay was named by ship's captains that cursed the sharp-edged rocks around the bay.

There are no marine facilities in Scarborough, however you can tie up to the long dock at the ferry terminal to fill up your water tanks, but check with someone in the *Port Authority* office first, they'll be glad to have somebody help you. Fuel anywhere in Tobago will have to be jerry-jugged.

Customs is located just to the right of the ferry terminal (east of the terminal) on the 2nd floor of the red-roofed building across from the pizza parlor. *Immigration* is located across the street from the ferry terminal on the 3rd floor of the *NIB* mall by *KFC*. The road in front of the ferry terminal, Carrington Street, is where you'll want to go to catch a taxi to anywhere on the island and there's a bus station up the road from the ferry dock behind the *KFC*. Next to *KFC* is a movie house, a great place to catch the latest flicks and enjoy how the Tobagans interact with the movie, they are certainly not content to sit back quietly and watch. Heading eastward along Carrington street you will pass several bars and restaurants and soon you will come to the *Cabin Pub* and *King's Well*, the former site of the town's main watercourse and now a bar and restaurant of the same name. Take a sharp right on

Castries Street and there is a steep road, Burnett Street, the center of knick-knack shopping in Scarborough. On the other side of town, a good walk west of the ferry docks, is the *East Ocean* restaurant.

At *NIB Mall*, sometimes called the *Scarborough Mall*, located just opposite the ferry dock, is where you go to find banks, a post office, pharmacies, a food court, and a library offering free Internet access as well as the latest periodicals and lots of history books on Trinidad and Tobago. Next to the mall is the *Scarborough Market*, a great place to find fresh fruits, vegetables, fish, and other local foods on Friday and Saturday mornings. Do not miss this market, it is a real treat.

Adjoining the mall is the *Botanical Gardens*, a great place to stop for a breather amid all the hustle and bustle of the street vendors and shoppers. Here on the 18-acre grounds of an old sugar estate, you can walk amid many species of flora that are indigenous to Tobago, but that are hard to find in the wild. The plants and trees are labeled and there's even a small fish pond graced by a statue created by Luise Kimmee, a well-known German sculptor who resides nearby.

High above the eastern side of the bay sits Fort King George, built by the British in 1779 and later captured by the French. The fort offers a magnificent view of Scarborough and Rockly Bay, and if you look to the east, you can see as far as Barcolet on the Windward Coast (what you might be inclined to call the "southern" coast). Visitors to the fort can view the old chapel, what's left of a prison, a cemetery, and can visit a craft shop. The *Museum of Tobago History* is located in the Barrack Guard House at Fort George and offers several nice exhibits showcasing Tobago's history ranging from pre-Columbian Amerindian artifacts to tableware once used by pirates and colonial settlers as well as some African drums and other period pieces.

Heading east from Scarborough on Bacolet Street you'll find some of the best restaurants in Scarborough. First is *Rouselle's*, ashore walk east of town. The balcony view of the harbor is a great backdrop for dinner as they are only open in the afternoons from around 3pm to 11pm. A bit further east is the *Old Donkey Cart House*, home to some great creole food and imported German wines, but I warn you, it might not fit well on some folk's budget. The restaurant is owned by Gloria Jones Schoen, a former German model who suggests reservations.

Just beyond is Bacolet, where The Beatles enjoyed a stay in the 60's. Here too you'll find *The Cotton House*, a studio set in an old colonial house where you can view beautiful batiks and if you're so inclined, can create your own to take with you, they'll show you how. If lovely Bacolet Bay Beach looks familiar let me remind you that it was used in the Disneyi film *Swiss Family Robinson*.

Folks wishing to tour a bit inland should visit nearby Mason Hall to view the beautiful 50' high Mason Falls.

CROWN POINT TO PIGEON POINT

Crown Point lies at the extreme southwestern tip of Tobago. It is home to Tobago's airport, several nice hotels, and a couple of good anchorages just north of the point at Store Bay and in Milford Bay off Pigeon Point. However, anchorages in the area between Crown Point and Pigeon Point are to be considered untenable in northerly swells that frequently occur during the winter months. The areas around Crown Point, Pigeon Point, Buccoo, Bon Accord, Mt. Pleasant, and almost all the way to Mt. Irvine, are known as the Lowlands situated as it is on the low lying coastal plain at the southwestern tip of Tobago.

Approaching Crown Point from Scarborough, follow the instructions in reverse (given in the last section, *Rockly Bay, Scarborough*) to work your way between the southwestern tip of Tobago and the shallow, and dangerous, Wasp Shoal as shown on Chart TOB-1. Round Crown Point a half-mile off and head for a waypoint at 11° 09.50' N, 60° 51.10' W, which places you approximately ½ mile west of the anchorage in Store Bay as shown on Chart TOB-3. Head in towards shore and anchor where your draft allows. This anchorage can be a bit rolly at times, and when the races are going on it may be full of power boats. During the world famous *Angostura/Yachting World Regatta*, which is usually held around the middle of May, Store Bay gets quite

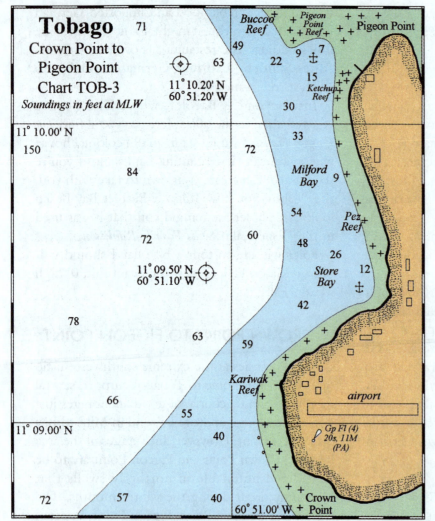

full and actually becomes a temporary Port of Entry for vessels wishing to clear in the week before the regatta. The regatta is open to all classes of sailboats from hard-core racers to liveaboard cruisers with all sorts of land based events to turn your attention to when you're not racing. Store Bay, named after an early Dutch settler named Jan Stoer, has one of the most popular beaches on the island. The coconut palms that you see are remnants of the days when the land around Store Bay was a coconut plantation.

North of Store Bay is another anchorage off Pigeon Point. As shown on Chart TOB-3, a GPS waypoint at 11° 10.20' N, 60° 51.20' W, will place you approximately ½ mile west of this anchorage. The anchorage itself lies generally west of the *Pigeon Point Resort*, between Pigeon Point Reef (part of the Buccoo Reef System) and Ketchup Reef. Holding is good in sand, but try not to drop the hook on any reef structure. Because the resort's beach is private, the resort requests that anchored yachts register with their office and pay a weekly fee for the use of their facilities. For TT$50 (at the time of this writing), you can use their garbage facilities, showers, and dinghy dock. Ice and water are available and the folks at *Viking Dive Shop* can help arrange propane and gasoline for you. The resort monitors VHF ch. 06 and *Viking* monitors ch. 71. You can dinghy around the point to Bon Accord Lagoon and some very good snorkeling (more on that in the next section on Buccoo Reef). Another good snorkel is Kariwak Reef, just off the beach west of the airport. The beach at the resort is as pretty as any beach to be found in the Caribbean and is often the subject of photographers, from the aquamarine waters of the Caribbean to the wooden pier and thatch-roofed huts backed by graceful palm trees.

Crown Point is the hub of tourism in Tobago. The airport is located here as well as several very nice hotels and quite a few car rental agencies. Many tourists that fly in to Tobago never make it past this area as so much of what they desire is here. The area is rife with food stalls, restaurants, and bars with enough happy hours to entertain all visitors. Local cuisine is well represented in the rotis, crab and dumplin', macaroni pie with callaloo, and curry goat and vegetable that you'll find in any one of several eateries in the area. Just take a stroll ashore and chose from *Miss Jean's, Miss Trim's, Alma's, Silvia's, Miss Esmee's*, and *Joicy's* for the best in local style eating. The dining is much the same from stall to stall and you won't be unhappy with any particular choice. The nearby *Taxi Co-Op Cafe* offers generous portions of food at a good price and is a popular hangout. The *Columbus Snackette*, known as *Uncle C's*, just across from the airport is a great spot for flying-fish sandwiches, beer, and just liming, especially on the weekends. *Eleven Degrees North* sits off the Store Bay road and boasts

Mexican and Cajun flavored foods heavy on the jalepeno. Air-conditioned *Drifter's Pub*, next to *Dillon's Restaurant,* a busy seafood restaurant, is a favorite tourist haunt.

Internet access in the Crown Point area is not much of a problem, there are three access points that are only a short walk from the anchorage in Store Bay. At the airport you can use the computers at the *Tourism Office* while just across from the airport is the *Cyber Café* with several new computers. A rather unique place is the *Clothes Wash Café* just down Milford Road a short distance from the airport toward Scarborough. Here you can do your clothes as you surf, though I found the rates quite pricey, three times the rates in Chaguaramas. When I mentioned this to the lady in charge she offered me a discount from TT$15 for 15 minutes, to TT$10 since I was paying in cash. In comparison, the *Mariner's Office* at the *Crew's Inn Marina* in Chaguaramas only charges TT$5 for 15 minutes while other cyber stops in the Chaguaramas area sometimes offer specials of TT$10 for an hour of surfing. Perhaps this will change, we can only hope so. The *Original Pancake House* on Milford Road now houses Internet access also.

In the immediate area of Crown Point you can get groceries at *Jimmie's MiniMart* or at the *Francis Supermarket* located in the Crown Point Beach Hotel. The *Tropikist Hotel* has an excellent bar and restaurant right on the edge of Store Bay. Their pool features a private waterfall and swim-up bar. A wealth of local information can be found in the person of Allan Clovis, the owner of *Kariwak Village* (an eco-resort designated Tobago's *Top Tourism Award* winner in 1999—don't miss their Saturday night buffet). Allan knows all the best spots around and is happy to help with directions and suggestions. Ask Allan for directions to *Robinson Crusoe's Cave* off the Bon Accord Road past the airport at the southern extremity of Crown Point. And when you head off to the cave, take a minute or two and view the remains of Fort Milford. The fort was preceded by a Latvian settlement and later, a Dutch redoubt called *Belleviste*. What you see today is all that remains of the fort the British built here in 1777. Six cannon here point out to sea; five of them are British, and one is French, deposited here when the French had possession of Tobago between 1781–1793. Past the fort the road curves left and shortly after you pass the airport runway you will come to a hand-painted sign marking the turn to the cave. Head to the last house and see Mrs. Crooks whose family owns the land which leads to the cave. She'll collect the TT$5 admission and direct you to the cave. The cave, once reaching all the way back to Store Bay, is now quite small, having been damaged over time by earthquakes.

It is said that after reading the novel *Robinson Crusoe,* Mr. Crooks came about the idea for the cave to coincide with the local rumor that Tobago was actually Crusoe's island. Although the author, Daniel Defoe, is said to have based his novel on the trials and tribulations of Alexander Selkirk on the island of Juan Fernandez off the coast of Chile, the introduction to the first edition places the hero in a different area entirely. Defoe's description describes the island of Robinson Cruise as lying off the Americas near the mouth of the river "Oroonoque." It is suggested that Defoe read a phamplet that was commissioned by the Duke of Courland describing the natural wonders of Tobago designed to entice developers to invest in Tobago. Some say that the descriptions in the phamplet gave Defoe a basis for his novel. Whatever the case may be, it's still a pretty spot.

If you head east on Milford Road, the principal highway between Scarborough and Crown Point, you'll find a great little cafe called the *Lion's Den* where you can have a cold drink, cappucino, a choice of appetizers, and a great dessert. Nearby is the *Fortune City Chinese Restaurant* as well as a Jamaican diner, a *Penny Saver Supermarket*, and in View Port, the *View Port Market.* In the same area is *Mariner's Outboards* where you can pick up some basic marine supplies and have your *Mercury* or *Mariner* outboard serviced.

BUCCOO REEF AND BUCCOO BAY

Buccoo Reef was established as a restricted area in 1973 and the removal or harming of corals, shells, or sea life is prohibited as is anchoring except in the designated areas. It has taken over 10,000 years

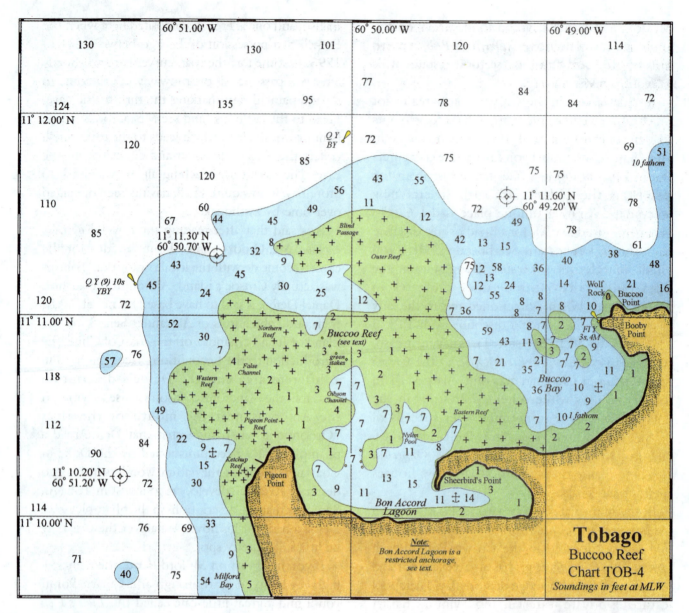

to create this masterpiece which is home to over 40 species of hard and soft corals. As shown on Chart TOB-4, the *Buccoo Reef* system is actually made up of several smaller reefs, of which the outer reefs dry at low water in places. The reefs are separated by three channels, *False Channel, Blind Passage,* and *Gibson Channel. Gibson Channel* the only one viable for cruising boats of any draft is sometimes shown as *Deep Channel* on some charts, but everybody knows it as *Gibson Channel.* It's named after Ralph Gibson, probably the most experienced and knowledgeable mariner in all of Trinidad and Tobago. Although a lot of the *Buccoo Reef* system seems to be dying, there is still a lot of coral and marine life for you to view while snorkeling from your dinghy. *Ketchup Reef* lies just southwest of Pigeon Point and stretches about 200 yards south. The reef received its name from a large cargo of ketchup that was dumped on the reef when a cargo ship ran aground there.

The best way to access the reef system for snorkeling is by anchoring north of *Kethcup Reef* in the small anchorage off Pigeon Point Resort as shown on Chart TOB-3 and TOB-4. Another good anchorage is in Buccoo Bay as shown on TOB-4. Recently I've heard cruisers tell me that they were told they could not anchor in Buccoo Bay, but officials that I've spoken to have reassured me that Buccoo Bay is not a part of the *Buccoo Park System* and anchoring is allowed. If Buccoo Bays ever becomes a part of the *Buccoo Reef National Park*, anchoring will not be permitted. For more information you can call the *Marine Park Manager* at 639-4446 or call the Park patrol on VHF ch. 16

As shown on TOB-4, a GPS waypoint at 11° 11.60' N, 60° 49.20' W, will place you approximately ½ mile north of the entrance to Buccoo Bay between Booby Point and Buccoo Reef. If approaching from the anchorages in the Store Bay area, give Buccoo Reef a wide berth. From the waypoint, steer generally SSE into the bay, heading generally for the rocky patch in the middle of the beach, and favoring the Buccoo Bay side to avoid the shallows off Booby Point. Once past the shoals off Booby Point turn to port and anchor off the beach wherever your draft allows. The beach, though pretty, is not a good spot for swimming, especially the day after *Sunday School* when it is used as a huge urinal by the hordes of partygoers. You can tie your dinghy up to the small dock, but you'll need a stern anchor.

The best anchorage, a spot to be considered as a hurricane hole, is in Bon Accord Lagoon. Now the anchorage here IS part of the national park and anchoring is prohibited except in the event of a hurricane. This mangrove-lined cove has good holding in 10' and offers great protection from all directions. Entrance directions will be given here with the understanding that the anchorage is only to be used for shelter from a hurricane...it is best explored by dinghy from the Pigeon Point anchorage.

As shown on TOB-4, a GPS waypoint at 11° 11.30' N, 60° 50.70' W, will place you approximately ½ mile northwest of *Gibson Channel*, the entrance channel to Bon Accord Lagoon. You'll have to use your eyes to pilot through here, no waypoints can be given. If approaching from Pigeon Point, keep an eye out for *False Channel*, easily recognized, that dead ends quickly in the reef system. *Gibson Channel* on the other hand can accept a 4' draft a bit above low water, and 6'–7' at high water (remember that the tidal range in Tobago is rougly 3'). From the waypoint given, pilot your way through the deep water pocket until you pick up the line of green stakes leading into Bon Accord Lagoon. Keep these green stakes close to port as you proceed on the dogleg leading into Bon Accord Lagoon. Near the southern terminus of the stakes is one red stake to keep to starboard just before entering the cove. Bear in mind that any and all of these stakes may be missing for various reasons so use caution, go slow, and use your eyes. Never attempt this route at night, in times of bad visibility, or with a swell running, there is no room for error with coral on both sides of you. On the northern side of the Bon Accord Lagoon (named after the old Bon Accord sugar plantation), is a deserted strip of sand called No Man's Land, a great spot for a swim if the tour boats aren't around having a barbecue. Plans have been made for a huge resort in the area around Bon Accord Lagoon (most of the land surrounding the cove is private) so keep your eyes open for this.

Some of the best snorkeling in Tobago can be found on the many reefs that comprise the Buccoo Reef System. A popular spot is the *Nylon Pool*, a shallow spot only about 3' deep that lies atop a sandbar in the middle of the bay. The *Nylon Pool* is said to have been named by Princess Margaret in the 1950's when she remarked that the water was as clear as her nylon stockings. A lot of Buccoo Reef is dead and more still dying thanks to carelessly placed anchors, misguided fishing spears, and unscrupulous coral collectors. Today's glass-bottom-boat operators are helping out with the care and preservation of the reef by only anchoring on dead coral and reminding their charges not to touch the reef or remove any corals. A three-hour tour on one of these boats only costs about TT$60 and takes three hours including a dip in the *Nylon Pool*.

The town of Buccoo is primarily a small fishing village where you can still purchase fresh fish along the beach. The residents are slowly getting away from fishing as they discovered the burgeoning tourist industry thanks to Buccoo Reef and glass bottom boats. Buccoo is known for several things, the most famous of which is *Sunday School*, a massive party packed with Tobagans and tourists. The festivities begin each Sunday evening around 8pm with live *Pan* music for a couple of hours. The crowd thickens by 10 or 11 P.M. as the sound systems from the beach stalls compete with each other to see who can achieve the highest decibel level as merrymakers sing and dance into the wee morning hours. A good spot to view the festivities is at the *Hendrix Hideaway*, especially during Easter when the biggest *Sunday School* of the year occurs with parked cars seemingly backed up as far as Mr. Irvine. The other event for which Buccoo is noted, are the Easter Tuesday goat races that were introduced by Barbadian Samuel Callender in 1825 as a poor man's substitute for horse racing. Racing goats, like horses, are a breed apart from their fellow goats and are never intended for the pot. They are sleek and graceful and bettors study them as their counterparts at the *Kentucky Derby* would a thoroughbred filly. The jockeys, who must be good sprinters, are tethered to their charges and attired in colorful vests and white shorts. The crowd feels the tension as the goats reach the manually operated starting gate. As the race begins the jockey's spur on their steeds with the help of a long stick, but unfortunately, and quite to the delight of the crowd, some goats take off on a tangent tripping up other goats and jockeys. The betting is heavy on this event as well as the accompanying crab races and everybody has fun. The scoreboard for the goat race is left up for the rest of the year to inspire the next year's contestants.

In town you can dine in any of several nice restaurants such as *La Tartaruga*, a fine Italian restaurant offering terrace dining and a cafe bar, but only for dinner. *Papillon*, at the *Old Grange Inn*, offers elegant and pricey dining in an open-air setting. *Teaside* offers great pizza in an informal atmosphere. *Baynes Seafood House* serves up some excellent local seafood every day except Thursday and is especially popular on Sundays just before *Sunday School* in Buccoo. *Esse's* is a small grocery store just down the road, and if you would like some great cold cuts and deli meats, try *R.T. Morshead* on the Buccoo Road in nearby Mt. Pleasant.

A nice sidetrip is a visit to Signal Hill, a great vantage point from which you can view the lowlands from Crown Point to Grafton Bay. Signal Hill was once used as a lookout location where observers could signal the nearby forts of approaching vessels. Today the area is home to a school and the Trinidad and Tobago Regiment whose marching band can sometimes be heard practicing. Nearby Orange Hill Road will take you up to Patience Hill where you can have a great view of the lowlands at Patience Hill Back Bottom Road.

If you'd like to charter a catamaran with a knowledgeable skipper, call *Loafer Cruises* at 639-7312. Their name says it all about their cruises. You'll get all you can eat and drink, and plenty of time to hang out, lime, and loaf. The *Nylon Pool* is one of their most popular stops.

MT. IRVINE BAY

Lying just northeast of Buccoo Bay are two good anchorages at Mt. Irvine Bay and Grafton Bay. If headed for Mt. Irvine Bay from Buccoo Bay, round Wolf Rock (TOB-4) giving it a berth of at least ¼ mile, heading for the northeastern tip of Mt. Irvine Bay to anchor in the lee of Rocky Point as shown on Chart TOB-5. If approaching from offshore head for a waypoint at 11° 11.80' N, 60° 48.60' W, which will place you approximately ½ mile west/northwest of the anchorage area. Head in towards the anchorage giving Rocky Point and its off-lying reef a wide berth.

Ashore in the center of the bay is the *Mt. Irvine Hotel* built on the site of a sugar plantation owned by Charles Irvine in the latter 1700's. The resort boasts the island's only golf course and cruisers are welcome to come ashore, pay a fee, and enjoy 18 holes or a few sets on the tennis court. The necessary equipment is available for rent (after all, how many cruising boats carry golf clubs aboard?). The championship golf course opened in 1968, and has been rated as one of the top fifty courses in the world. You are welcome to use the beach at the hotel and take a shower if you buy a drink at the bar.

Mt. Irvine Beach is a favorite stop for tourists and locals alike. Ashore you'll find gazebos, palm trees, and beach facilities (showers!) that charge TT$1. Surfers flock here in the winter months when northerly swells create good surfing opportunities. This is why you'll spy the *Surfer's Restaurant and Bar* on the shore. There are also several arts and crafts shops and the *Waterfront Restaurant*, home of some of the best *Shark n' Bake* on the island. A half-mile to the northeast you will find a telephone, a tourism kiosk with a car rental, and a bank with an *ATM*.

At the northern tip of Mt. Irvine Bay is Rocky Point, and off the point you'll find great snorkeling on *Mt. Irvine Reef*, sometimes called *Mt. Irvine Wall*, and that should give you an idea of what you'll find on that dive. Further out from the point is the wreck of the *Maverick*, another interesting dive site. On the northern side of Rocky Point is a small beach known as Back Bay, a popular nude beach.

In the hills across the road from the beach is the *Kimmee Museum*, the private gallery of German-born sculptress Luise Kimmee. Kimme moved to Tobago in 1979, and set up a studio with local sculptor and fisherman Albert Prince. Her 12' tall wooden carvings, fashioned from tree trunks, depict Tobagan dancing and various creatures of folklore such as the *Soucouyant* and *La Diablesse*. The museum is only open on Sundays from 11–2 and is free. If you wish to visit at other times call 639-0257 for an appointment.

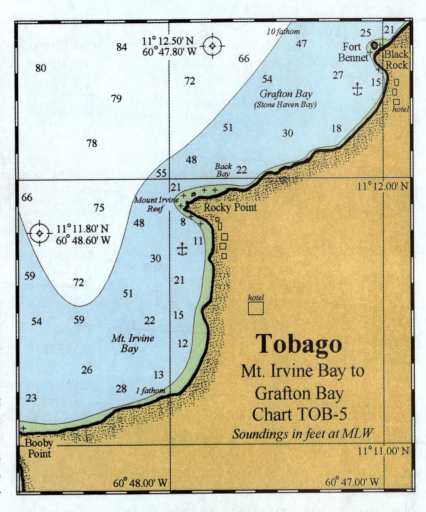

GRAFTON BAY

The next anchorage that we will visit on our circumnavigation is Grafton Bay, often called Stone Haven Bay and sometimes shown on charts as such. Approaching from Mt. Irvine Bay is easy, it's just around the corner so to speak. As shown on Chart TOB-5, give Rocky Point a wide berth and head toward the anchorage area off the beach just inside the point at Black Rock. If approaching from offshore a GPS waypoint at 11° 12.50' N, 60° 47.80' W, will place you approximately ¾ mile WNW of the anchorage area. Head in towards the beach giving a wide berth to the point at Black Rock and round up to anchor off the posh *Grafton Beach Resort*. The anchorage can be quite rolly and dinghies should land at the extreme northern end of the beach.

The *Grafton Beach Resort* stands on the grounds of the old Grafton estate once owned by the Smith family, a family with a long history on Tobago. Don't miss the Friday night barbecue complete with live music.

If you take a short walk south on the main road you find the entrance to *The Sanctuary* or more precisely, the *Grafton Caledonia Wildlife Sanctuary*. After Hurricane Flora hit Tobago in 1963, Eleanor Alefounder began a bird feeding program at her cocoa estate since the animals had found themselves short of food after the damage that Flora wrought. This daily feeding snowballed into a bird sanctuary and Mrs. Alefounder left a clause in her will designating this part of her estate to remain a sanctuary. Today, you can enter the grounds and visit James Sampson, the "Bird Man," who is the caretaker of the estate and an authority on Tobago avian life. The estate has several marked trails that you can stroll to view birds such as bananaquits, cocrico, mot-mots, and

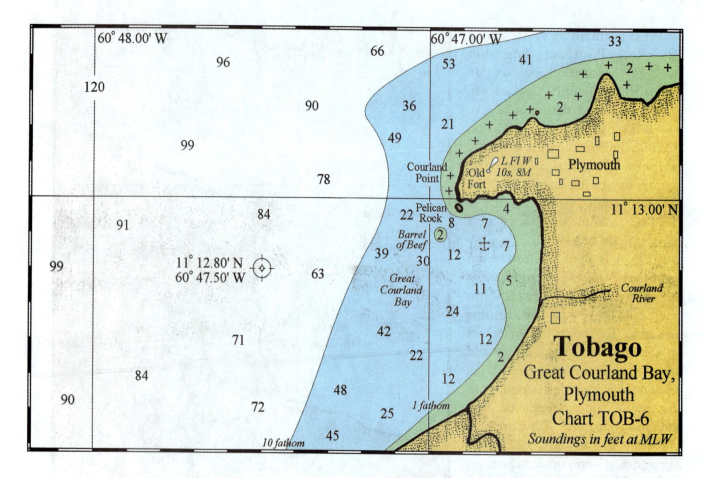

blue tanagers (blue jays). Try to get there for the 4pm feeding at the Copra House. Just south of the Sanctuary is *Marie's Mini Mart* in Pleasant Prospect, a good spot for some basic groceries. Across the street from *Marie's* is the *Two Season's Restaurant* which offers great pizza and vegetarian delights. Next door is *The Emerald* with good food in a breezy upstairs setting.

Heading north on the main road you'll find the settlement of Black Rock with several nice rum shops (bars). The *Black Rock Cafe*, an open-air restaurant that sits on the outskirts of Black Rock, serves breakfast, lunch, and dinner. In town you can find the *Mon Cheri Cafe*, *Michael's*, and a small supermarket. To seaward of Black Rock are the remains of Fort Bennet, built by British Lt. Robert Bennet in 1680. The British expanded Fort Bennet during the plantation era in 1778 to protect against American privateers during the American Revolution. Today the fort offers great views of the surrounding waters as well as particularly nice sunsets.

■ GREAT COURLAND BAY, PLYMOUTH

Great Courland Bay and the town of Plymouth have a long and confusing history. The British originally settled Tobago in 1625 when the first group of settlers were wiped out by the indigenous Amerindians. In 1628, the Dutch arrived at Plymouth, but a combined force of Indians and Spaniards from Trinidad arrived in canoes and killed off the Dutch settlers, the only time that Trinidad and Tobago ever went to war with each other. In 1639, the British arrived again, only to be run off once more by the Amerindians. Tiring of this, Charles I gave the island to his godson, Duke James Jekabs of Courland (Latvia), and another settlement was established at Plymouth in 1642 by the Courlanders. Again, the settlers made like a ping-pong ball being chased off by the Indians, returning in 1650, and again in 1654. In 1658, the Dutch returned and claimed dominion of the island and renamed the settlement *Nieuw Vissingen*. Twenty years later the remaining Courlanders left, but some of their Latvian descendants still make an annual pilgrimage to Plymouth. In Plymouth you can view

Fort James, Grand Courland Bay, Tobago.

The Courland Monument, a striking sculpture unveiled in 1976 that commemorates the 17th century settlers from Latvia.

The Dutch finally were driven off by the British, who had built a fort atop Courland Point. The British had maintained a military presence at Plymouth, which was now the Capital of Tobago. With an excellent view of the Grand Courland Bay, Fort James sits atop Courland Point, its cannon still pointing to sea. The fort was built by the British in 1768 during the plantation era as a barracks for the troops sent to protect the settlement at Plymouth (the British were also constructing several other forts on Tobago at this time as well). Named after the Duke of Courland, James Jekabs, the fort has an interesting history. Once again the ping-pong ball was to bounce as the French arrived. A nighttime insertion of two dozen French soldiers was the key to French victory at Plymouth. The soldiers made such a ruckus the next morning that the confused British though they were outnumbered. The French commander notified his British counterpart there were a thousand Frenchmen waiting to attack on his signal which terrified the British leader to surrender immediately with no shots fired. The conquering French destroyed the settlements and quickly abandoned the island. Luckily for us this was not the end of the story and so today you'll find a friendly residential community sitting atop the ridge overlooking the bay.

If you're leaving Grafton Bay, simply give the point at Black Rock and its off-lying rock a wide berth, at least ¼ mile off, and head straight for the northeastern pocket of Great Courland Bay. Vessels arriving from offshore can head for a GPS Waypoint at 11° 12.80' N, 60° 47.50' W, which will place you approximately ½ mile west of the anchorage area as shown on Chart TOB-6. From the waypoint head a bit south of east giving the shoal off Courland Point a wide berth to round up and drop the hook just southeast of the fort atop Courland Point. Don't try to pass between the submerged rock known as *Barrel of Beef* and

Rafael Anslim Davis is a busker, a Calypso Poet, someone who improvises Calypso, at Great Courland Bay, Tobago.

Pelican Rock. The bottom is rocky here and only 8'–11' deep in spots, it's best to avoid it and *Barrel of Beef*, you really don't gain anything by passing inside the submerged rock, and you put a lot at risk.

The curving beach that you see is known as Turtle Beach. During the months from March to August huge leatherback turtles come ashore to lay their eggs. In just a little over thirty minutes they will dig a hole straight down 3' deep and deposit their eggs, two or three at a time. When they cover the nest and leave, you will hardly know they were ever there, so well do they recover the spot. Within six weeks, the hatchlings begin making their way to sea to someday return to lay their eggs on the beach.

Midway down the beach you'll find the *Turtle Beach Hotel* whose facilities are for their guests only, however feel free to visit the *Kiskadee Restaurant* with its nightly live entertainment and ever changing schedule of buffets and barbecues.

In Plymouth there are several small grocery stores with the usual basic provisions as well as a gas station if you don't mind jerry-jugging your fuel. You can get a bite to eat at the *Cocorite Inn* or the more laid back, *Sunset Restaurant*.

Taking a hike up to Courland Point to visit the fort you'll likely meet Rafael Davis. Rafael Anslim Davis is a *busker*, a *Calypso Poet*, someone who improvises *Calypso* for money. A *busker* must be able to improvise, to think quickly on his feet, and make up humorous verses for you that will entice you to part with a blue one (a TT$100 note), and Rafael is very good at it. Give him a listen, you can't help that, he'll sing for you whether you want him to or not. Then you decide if you think he's worth a blue one.

Just a bit northeast of the fort is the *Mystery Tombstone*. The tombstone, dated 1783, marks the double grave of 23-year old Betty Stiven and her child. The mystery is the tombstone's inscription which states: "What was remarkable of her, she was a mother without knowing it, and a wife without letting her husband know it, except by her kind indulgencies to him." Betty is said to have been the African maid and lover of wealthy Dutch planter Alex Stiven. Local experts will give you two stories concerning the inscription. One theory is that Betty gave birth to Alex's mixed-blood child and he took charge of the infant raising it as his own and not acknowledging Betty as the mother, leaving her free to remain as his lover, making her a mother without knowing it. The other theory suggests that the affair between Betty and Alex was highly secret as Alex could not be seen as having a slave as a lover. When Betty died at childbirth Alex is said to have created the inscription as a testament of his love for her. Take your pick, I personally believe the latter . . . but who knows? That's why it's a mystery.

Just north of Plymouth is Culloden Bay, shallow and reef strewn, I only mention if for the fantastic diving available there. Here you'll find a tremendous amount of coral structure and waters rich in diverse marine life that is virtually untouched by man. It has been recommended that Culloden Bay be designated a Marine Reserve, a good idea to protect

Great Courland Bay, Tobago.

this beautiful area. Culloden Bay is home to *Footprints*, an eco-friendly resort whose focus is the preservation and protection of the environment. The rooms are perched on stilts and have solar heated Jacuzzis built of teak and recycled hardwoods. Another mile or so northeastward is Arnos Vale Bay, also shallow with access only for small fishing boats via a narrow, shallow channel. Arnos Vale Bay is another one of the great snorkeling sites located on the northern coast of Tobago.

If you're driving through the area you will notice that the roads through here are quite pleasant as you proceed north of Plymouth. They are well paved with few potholes, narrow and steep in places, in others the sharp curves are lined with large concrete walls and curbs. You'll pass lots of sheer drop-offs with breathtaking views of the Caribbean, the mountains and valleys of the rain forest, and several hilltop settlements. In places you'll drive through huge bamboo canopies and both sides of the roads are thick with jungle-like vegetation as you run alongside a fresh-water stream.

On the road outside Plymouth there are pineapple shaped signs that read "Follow the pineapple to the *Arnos Vale Waterwheel*." If you follow the signs you'll soon find the waterwheel, but first you need to make a stop at the *Adventure Farm and Nature Reserve* for some birdwatching and guided tours of its 12 acres.

Following the pineapples you'll continue along amid all sorts of tropical vegetation and soon come to the *Arnos Vale Waterwheel Park*, an absolutely gorgeous place. This entire area was once the Arnos Vale sugar plantation and today little is left save the beach resort at Arnold Vale Beach and the *Waterwheel Park*. At the park you can stroll along a wooden walkway and view the restored remains of the old waterwheel that powered the old mill, and the steam train that moved sugar cane around the estate. There is a very nice restaurant with a buffet every Wednesday and Friday, a gift shop along with a small museum and theater with exhibits of Amerindian and colonial artifacts. Take a walk through the grounds and view the sweet scented tropical plants and colorful flowers that the former

British owners of this estate planted on the grounds.

If you continue past *Waterwheel Park* you'll come to a crossroads at Les Couteaux. Taking a left will allow you to continue along the northern coast with its stunning vistas. Taking a right will take you into Scarborough, and if you continue straight ahead you'll come to the *Hillsborough Dam* where there's a good chance you might see a caiman as they like to lime in the still waters above the dams on Tobago and Trinidad. The town of Les Couteaux itself is known locally for the fact that *Obeah* is said to still be practiced here, *Obeah* being a form of magic that originated in Africa. During the *Heritage Week Festival* every July the town hosts scary storytelling sessions for those interested.

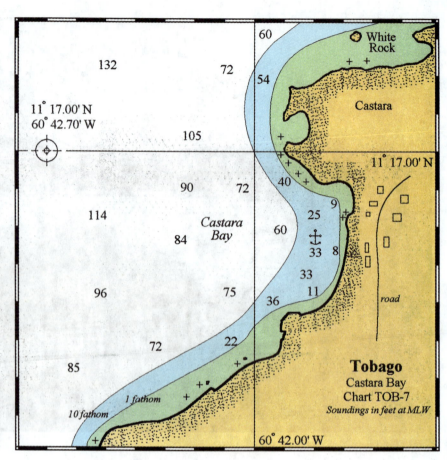

■ CASTARA BAY

Your next stop on your circumnavigation can be Castara Bay as shown on Chart TOB-1. If headed there from Great Courland Bay, keep at least a half-mile offshore to avoid any off-lying dangers. Yes, I know, other guides say you can keep in as close as ¼ mile, but I suggest a more conservative approach just to be on the safe side, the choice is up to you. Head for a waypoint at 11° 17.00' N, 60° 42.70' W, which places you approximately ½ mile west/northwest of the anchorage area off the public beach as shown on TOB-7.

Castara is a small fishing village whose 500 or so inhabitants fish and farm, though a few work for the government in a series of seemingly never-ending road improvement projects. The popular public beach has some very nice changing facilities with showers along with the *Cascreole Restaurant and Bar* where you are invited to try *Bobo Shanty's* herbal steam bath. Along the working section of the beach you'll find fishermen liming away, mending their nets and waiting for the tide to change. The *Fisherman's Co-Op* (the building where the fishermen clean their catch) is a good place to buy some fresh fish and the small restaurant directly behind it a great spot for a really satisfying and economical meal.

Castara is a good spot to see fisherman seine netting. Seine netting, or *pulling seine*, is the Tobagan communal fishing method and you're likely to see it anywhere in the anchorages of the island. Fishermen drop nets in a circle from the shore by small boat and anybody and everybody is welcome to haul in the net and payment is made in fish. In August the town celebrates the *Castara Fisherman's Fete* with party-goers eating, drinking, and dancing from noon until late into the night.

Everything here is built on the hillsides overlooking beautiful Castara Bay. If you need groceries there are several small stalls set up along the roadside to sell basic supplies. Henry Jackson's *First and Last* roti stand is just up the road from the beach with good rotis, rum, and a few sundry supplies. There's also the

Castara Bay, Tobago.

No Problem food store nearby as well as the *L&H Sunset Restaurant* next to the *Fisherman's Co-Op* (beneath the *L&H* is a small food store).

Just outside of town heading north are the *Naturalist Beach Resort* (Do you think the name implies what you'll find here? You're wrong! It is for those who are into nature and a *No Nudity* sign was put up when people began getting the wrong idea about the place.) and *Aleisha's Video Club* for movie rentals.

At the eastern edge of Castara is a bridge over the Castara River. If you follow the river upstream for about 15 minutes you'll find a small waterfall with a deep pool at the bottom for swimming. There's another waterfall about an hour's walk away and the best way to find it is to hire a local guide such as Hilly Williams (639-6485).

▪ ENGLISHMAN'S BAY

A little further along the northern coast is one of my favorite spots, serene and secluded Englishman's Bay. From Castara keep ½ mile offshore and head for a waypoint at 11° 18.00' N, 60° 40.80' W, which places you approximately ½ mile northwest of the anchorage area as shown on Chart TOB-8. Head in toward the beach and anchor on the eastern side of the bay. If you see some fishermen seine netting from a small boat, don't get in their way, better to anchor elsewhere until they're finished. An option is to anchor in the southern part of the bay until the fisherman have beached their catch, but if it's too uncomfortable there move on, either back to Castara Bay or northward to Parlatuvier Bay. Either way, the anchorage along the eastern shore can be rolly at times also. Ashore, *Eula's* offers hot meals (rotis on Sundays), cold drinks, and hand-made crafts at the small stall with outside tables.

Englishman's Bay is part of the *Englishman's Bay State Nature Reserve*, but all this may change. I've learned that plans have been made for a large hotel resort on the beach, but luckily nothing concrete has begun as of this writing.

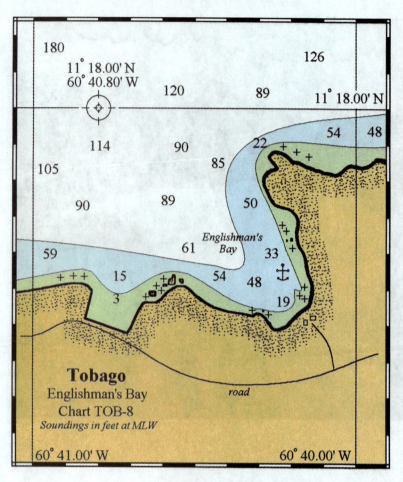

PARLATUVIER BAY

Parlatuvier Bay, snug and small, offers very good protection and a large dock to access the shore (and also pick up some fresh water). As shown on Chart TOB-9, a GPS waypoint at 11° 18.23' N, 60° 39.30' W, which places you approximately ½ mile northwest of the anchorage area. From the waypoint head into the bay, giving the point and its adjacent reef a wide berth and anchoring off the pier so as not interfere with the local fishing craft. Keep an eye out for seine netting in the southern part of Parlatuvier Bay. The beach is sometimes used by leatherback turtles when nesting.

Parlatuvier is another one of those quaint northern-shore fishing villages as is evident by the fleet colorful pirogues moored off the beach. As you gaze at your surroundings you'll notice the entire settlement is carefully placed and terraced on the hillsides surrounding this lovely bay. Ashore you'll find a small gift shop and Duran Chance's small grocery store where you can pick up a few groceries, re-supply your rum locker, and access a card phone. At *Bryner and Gloria's Riverside Restaurant* on the Northside Road you can dine on healthy portions of locally caught fish while just a bit further east you can pick up a good roti at *Apache Cottage*. A short walk up the road from the dock will bring you to a small waterfall.

If you are traveling by car through here, you'll have to take the turnoff here that leads through the rain forest to Roxborough as the road along the northern shore ends abruptly just past Parlatuvier. Only the best of four-wheel drive vehicles and drivers can make it further east along the coast to Charlotteville. So few attempt this that the sight of a tourist in the tiny settlement of L'Anse Fourmi is a rarity for the locals.

Parlatuvier is a good base for trips to the rain forest. Heading for Roxborough you'll pass through the *Tobago Forest Reserve*, a tropical rain forest high in the central mountains of Tobago. The oldest protected forest reserve in the New World, the forest was designated a reserve in 1776. One of the best spots to view the forest is at Gilpin Trace, marked by a huge rock slab on the road in front of the *Forestry* hut where you'll find a toilet and water tank. On weekends you can get snacks and drinks here from local vendors. Hikers can follow a trail into the rain forest from here, but it is recommended that they hire a guide, and only a card-carrying licensed guide. One of the best is Renson Jack (660-5175). Renson is a *Forest Ranger* who moonlights as a guide and he is highly knowledgeable about the local fauna and flora. Other guides worthy of a recommendation are David Brooks (660-5175), and Harris McMillan (639-6575).

A few miles down the road to Roxborough you'll come to another *Forestry* hut where local guides

Parlatuvier Bay, Tobago.

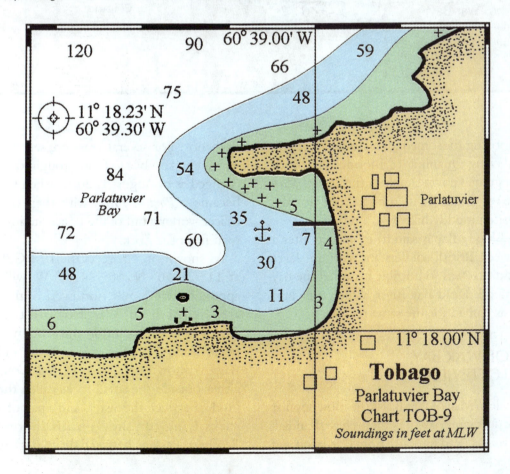

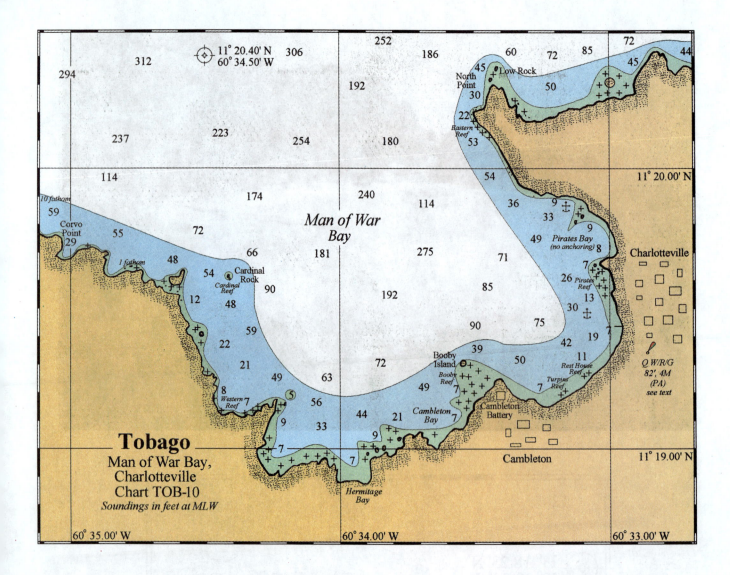

hang out looking for someone to guide. Here you can hire Fitzroy Quanima of Bloody Bay (660-7836) or a guide known simply as the *Parrot Man* (639-1305) who also rents rubber boots for the long and often muddy hikes.

Nearby Bloody Bay is said to be named after a battle between British soldiers and African slaves in 1771 and that was so horrible it turned the bay red with blood. Dead Bay River, which runs into the bay, was named for the same reason.

■ MAN OF WAR BAY, CHARLOTTEVILLE

Charlotteville in Man of War Bay is the most popular stop on the northern coast, it is the preferred landfall for many cruisers heading south from Carriacou and Barbados. For several years cruisers could anchor here and take a bus to Scarborough to clear in. This changed as of August 1, 2001, when Charlotteville became a *Port of Entry* with their own *Customs* officer working out of the Police Station just up the road from the dock.

As shown on Chart TOB-10, a GPS waypoint at 11° 20.40' N, 60° 34.50' W, will place you approximately 1 mile northwest of the anchorage area in Man of War bay off the town of Charlotteville. A caution must be made here for boats heading to Man of War Bay from Parlatuvier Bay. As shown on Chart TOB-1, you must pass either outside the small rocks called the Sisters or inside, between the Sisters and a pair of submerged rocks lying off the Tobago shore called the Brothers. Passage between the two is deep and easy

Englishman's Bay, Tobago.

if the Brothers are breaking making their position quite conspicuous. If they're not breaking, favor the Sisters side of the channel and keep your eyes open. For your information, although I do not recommend the inside passage at night, the Sisters are lit (Fl (2) W 10s, 8M).

From the waypoint at Man of War Bay proceed into the bay heading toward the dock in Charlotteville at the southeastern corner of the bay. As shown on TOB-10 you can anchor off the dock in 30'–60' of water off the town dock southwest of Pirates Reef (keep clear of the moored pirogues), or in the small cove north of Pirates Bay northwest of the two off-lying rocks. You cannot however, anchor in Pirates Bay or off the beach as these areas are used for seine netting. It is possible to anchor in Cambleton Bay, to the west of Charlotteville, but the holding is poor in rock and the area uncomfortable except in the calmest of conditions

Ashore you'll find lots of amenities to please almost any cruiser. Tie up to the dock and directly across the road is the *Bayview Shopping Mart*, a good stop for groceries. Also at the head of the dock is *Eastman's Restaurant*. Charlotteville is a fisherman's village and on the west side of the dock is the fishermen's co-op for those who want fresh fish, if fact, 60% of the fish brought into Tobago come in through Charlotteville. All around the dockside area are several small shacks where you can get a bite to eat. On the other side of town *Sharon and Phebe's Restaurant* serves up breakfast, lunch, and dinner on their balcony, and can also arrange to take care of your laundry needs. The beach has public changing areas and showers (TT$1). In Pirate's Bay you'll find a small stream trickling down into the bay and offering a fresh water shower. Climb the 150 concrete steps and you'll be on a small dirt road leading into town.

Just up the road from the dock, under the large antenna tower, you'll find the *Charlotteville Health Center*, the Police Department, *Customs* office, and the public library which offers a free half-hour of Internet access. If you join the library for TT$10 you'll have greater access to the library's computers. Internet access is also available at the *Charlotteville Beach Bar and Restaurant*. If you

Man of War Bay, Charlotteville, Tobago.

want ice cream you're in luck. Every afternoon Shielah walks down to the dock with a wooden bucket full of ice cream, keep an eye out for her. If you need to rent a car call *George's Rentals* at 639-8295. Route taxis run into Roxborough and Scarborough for those needing better shopping than that offered in Charlotteville. A gas station in town sells diesel, gasoline, and kerosene, but you'll have to jerry-jug it (I'll bet you're tired of hearing that, aren't you?). On the road behind the *Man of War Bay Cottages* you'll find the *Golden Dove Restaurant* where you can choose from several local dishes.

Charlotteville is a lovely town, probably the most picturesque town on the island of Tobago, where houses are perched on steep hillsides with narrow streets running here and there and winding paths heading up into the hills. The bay area was first settled by Carib Indians and later by the Dutch who, in 1633, named the bay Jan De Moor Bay after one of the residents. During the plantation years the area was divided into two estates, Charlotteville and Pirates Bay. In 1865, both estates were purchased by the Turpin family who still own much of the surrounding land.

The road out of town is long and steep, but the views are stunning from the crest atop Flagstaff Hill just off the main road. Here you'll find an old signalman's hut and pylon topped with a navigational beacon. This outpost was used by British and French soldiers who used mirrors to signal the approach of a ship to their comrades at the Cambleton Battery below. Cambleton Battery was built by the British in 1777 to defend against American privateers working the waters of the Caribbean during the American Revolution.

Good snorkeling abounds in Man of War Bay. *Pirates Reef* is shallow and offers some excellent coral structures, but watch out for the fire coral. At the southern end of the bay, lying just southeast of the extensive *Booby Reef* and just off the shoreline, lie *Turpins Reef* and *Rest House Reef*. *Booby Reef* is gorgeous, lots of elkhorn coral and a steep slope to deeper water. Another nice spot is *Cardinal Reef* with its almost vertical drop to over 10 fathoms.

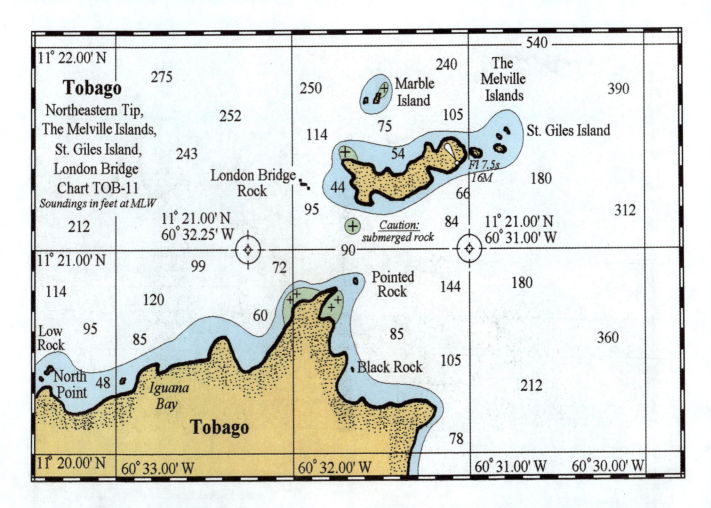

THE NORTHEASTERN TIP, THE MELVILLE ISLANDS

On Chart TOB-11, you'll notice the Melville Islands, comprised of several small islands such as St. Giles Island and London Bridge. On some charts these are shown as the St. Giles Islands, while on others they are simply called the Melvilles. In 1968, Charles Turpin, the proprietor of the Charlotteville Estate in northeastern Tobago, presented the Government of Tobago the Melville Islands to be used as a bird sanctuary. Due to the lack of predators, and the lack of man, the islands are able to support a large population of nesting seabirds, terns, boobies, frigate birds, and the uncommon tropic-bird.

The hairiest part of your circumnavigation of Tobago will be rounding the northeastern tip of Tobago. You have two choices here, either passing inside the Melville Islands, or passing outside the Melville Islands. I recommend the outside passage, but be advised that you will find yourself in a strong current of over two knots as you head north around Marble Island. This is generally not a problem and, you won't have to worry about submerged rocks like the one lying south of St. Giles Island. The outside route is just a little longer, it certainly won't delay you more than an hour or two when heading for Tyrrel's Bay and Speyside, so I suggest you take a few more tacks and enjoy the sailing. If you're not convinced, or if you have a good motor and the wind and seas are down, you can pass south of St. Giles Island.

As shown on TOB-11 a waypoint at 11° 21.00' N, 60° 32.25' W, will place you ½ mile west of the channel between St. Giles Island and Pointed Rock. Head eastward favoring the Pointed Rock side of the channel to avoid the submerged rock south of St. Giles Island. If there are any seas the rock will be breaking and easily seen, if not, use caution and keep your eyes open, watch for water turbulence to help you locate the rock. Never

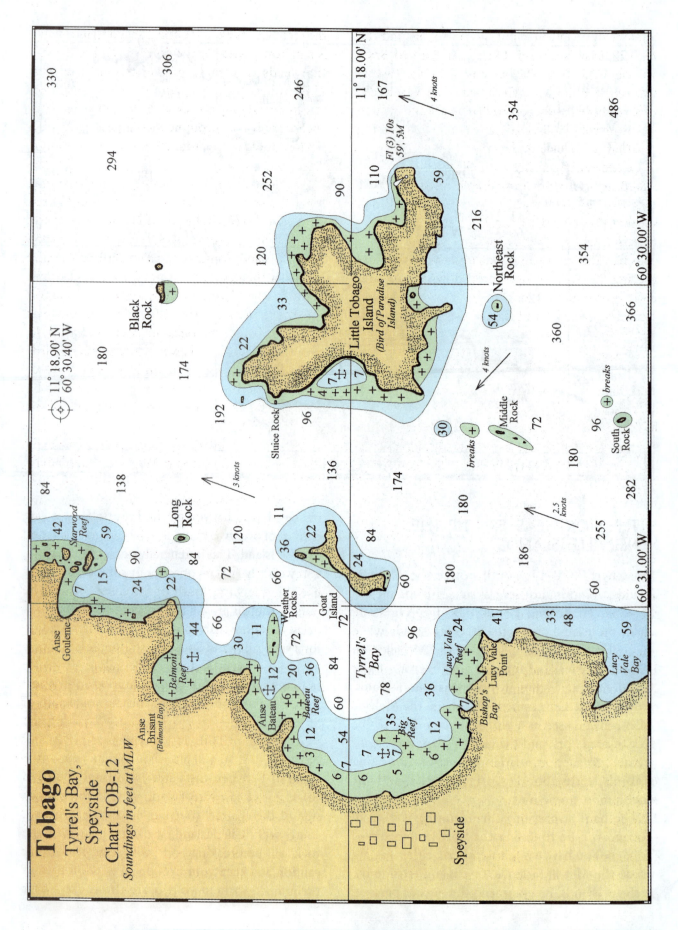

attempt this route at night, go north, around the Melville Islands instead. Once past Pointed Rock you can begin to work your way down the eastern side of the island, the Windward shore keeping ½ mile offshore as you approach Tyrrel's Bay. Watch out for strong and erratic currents when passing south of St. Giles Island.

London Bridge, lying just a bit west of St. Giles Island, is a naturally formed arch atop a pinnacle that rises from a depth of over 100'. You can snorkel through the arch, but caution must be exercised. Never try this with any sort of swell if possible. You can swim right through the arch and if using SCUBA, you can drop down to 80' and more to ride the current around the canyons and crevasses at the base of the pinnacle.

TYRREL'S BAY, SPEYSIDE

Tyrrel's Bay undoubtedly has some of the best snorkeling and a fairly good anchorage that doesn't look as good on paper as it really is. Vessels heading for the Tyrrel Bay area from the Melville Islands area can head for a waypoint at 11° 18.90' N, 60° 30.40' W, which places you ½ mile north/northeast of the entrance to Tyrrel's Bay between Long Rock and Little Tobago Island as shown on Chart TOB-12. From this waypoint take Long Rock to starboard to anchor in Anse Bateau just off the *Blue Waters Inn*. The anchorage is best accessed by passing between Weather Rocks and Goat Island and then turning to starboard to anchor in the bay. On paper it looks like this bay is open to the southeast, and it is to an extent, but Little Tobago Island, Goat Island, and Weather Rocks combine to diminish any seas. You can also anchor south of Anse Bateau just off the town of Speyside in the lee of Big Reef as shown on TOB-12. Vessels can anchor in Anse Brisant, just north of Anse Bateau, but it is more exposed and the reef prevents you from tucking up close to shore. There also is a small anchorage in the lee of Little Tobago Island, but it is difficult to get into, but if you can gain access, you'll likely be alone and the waters quite calm. Approach Little Tobago Island's western shore and head towards the northern end of the conspicuous green water which delineates the reef that lies west of Little Tobago Island. There is a narrow passage at the northern end of the reef that leads to a small pocket behind the reef. Unfortunately the passage is directly over reef structure and only carries 5'–6' at high water. This anchorage is not recommended unless you have a shallow draft and can sound your way in by dinghy first.

Goat Island's conspicuous house was once the holiday home of Ian Fleming, the creator of James Bond. The house and grounds are now private and visits ashore must be by invitation only. Little Tobago Island, sometimes called Bird of Paradise Island, is the easternmost point of Trinidad and Tobago. The island was once a cotton plantation and then, in the early 1900's, the island was purchased by ornithologist Sir William Ingram. In 1909 Ingram imported several dozen Greater Birds of Paradise from Aru Island in New Guinea. Over the years the bird population was decimated by hurricanes and poachers. After the death of Sir William in 1924, his heirs gave the island to the Government of Tobago with the proviso that the island be a protected area. It has remained a seabird colony ever since although you won't find any Birds of Paradise anywhere around. There are several trails on the island that date back to the plantation days and guides can be found in Speyside to give you the grand tour of the island. Landing on the small beach on the western side of the island you'll find a small hut with toilet and a list of do's and don'ts for visitors. Concrete steps lead up the hillside past the old caretaker's house and several trails branch off leading through the surround landscape. You could not find a more knowledgeable guide than David Rooks (639-4276), who once persuaded David Attenborough to include Little Tobago Island in his famous BBC documentary *Trials of Life*.

The *Blue Waters Inn* is a hub of activity in the Speyside area. An eco-friendly resort, the Inn offers 38 rooms set amid 46 lush acres and *The Tobago Dive Experience* is a great spot to begin a diving adventure in the surrounding waters. Tyrrel's Bay offers some of the best reef diving and snorkeling in the Trinidad/Tobago area and there are several dive shops and glass bottom boat tours for those

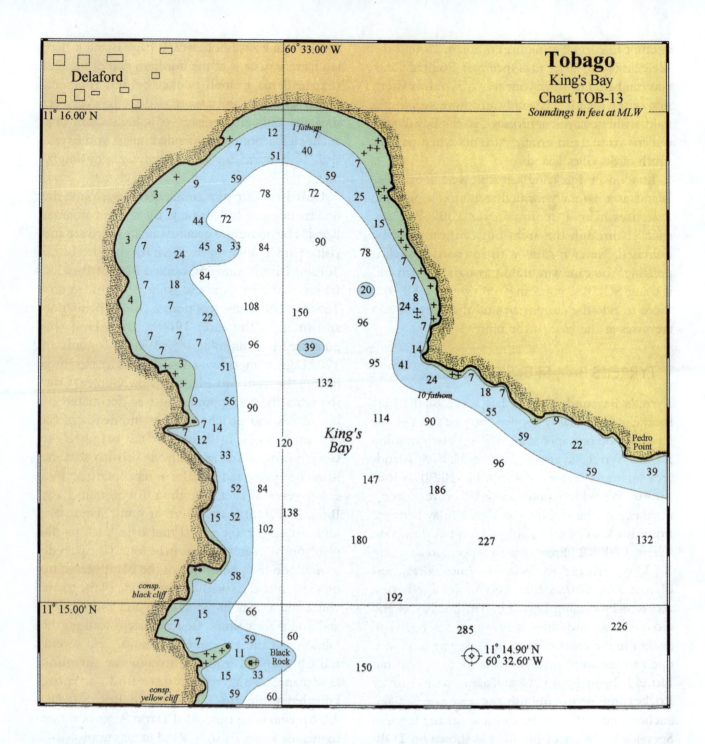

so inclined. The best reefs in the area are shown on Chart TOB-13 and can be used as guide to give you the general location of the best dive areas. Divers must be aware that there is a prevailing northerly current in Tyrrel's Bay and makes open water dives drift dives. Some of the best snorkeling is just off the beach at the *Blue Waters Inn*, Goat Island, Weather Rocks, and Little Tobago Reef that lies west and south of Little Tobago Island.

For more specific information, please see one of the local dive shops.

Northeast of the *Blue Waters Inn* you'll find the ruins of an old water wheel and a small stream that leads into the bay. In years past the wheel powered a mill and furnished water, and the stream was used as a fresh water bath. Visit their *Fish Pot Restaurant* for good, if not pricey, seafood.

Until a little over a decade ago, Speyside had

just one road and no tourism industry. Today the *Windward Highway* passes directly though the town connecting Charlotteville and Scarborough, and there are several inns and dive shops to accommodate tourists and dive aficionados. The public beach, like so many others on the island, has public changing and shower facilities and the nearby sports field is a focal point for the community. There are many small restaurants and dive shops that cater to tourists and divers alike, and are popular places to dine and lime. Here you'll find the *Speyside Beach Bar*, *Anthony's Dive Center*, the *Sunset Guest House*, the *Birdwatcher's Cafe*, the *Seafront Cafe*, *Black Pirate Seafood and Pizza House*, *Redman's Restaurant and Dive Center*, *Liz's Cafe and Bar*, and the most unique of all, *Jemma's Restaurant*, built into a tree overlooking the bay. In town you'll also find an *Ace Hardware*.

KING'S BAY

Picturesque King's Bay is a fair enough anchorage in most conditions save a strong southeasterly, but the bay come in to its own during the winter months when northerly swells make all Tobago anchorages except King's Bay and Scarborough untenable.

As shown on Chart TOB-13, a GPS waypoint at 11° 14.90' N, 60° 32.60' W, will place you approximately ½ mile southeast of the bay. Don't head to this directly to this waypoint unless well offshore as the waypoint does not allow for surrounding land. For instance, if you're approaching from Speyside, keep well offshore, at least ½ mile, until you round Pedro Point at which time you can head for the waypoint. From the waypoint head up into the bay and anchor off the eastern shore wherever your draft allows as shown on TOB-13.

Once a large Amerindian settlement, the folks that live here now reside in houses set high up on the hills well above the bay. Just south of the central part of the bay well up on the road is the *King's Bay Cafe* if you'd like a meal with a spectacular view.

At the northeastern corner of the bay is a public beach facility with showers. At the end of the beach is a small restaurant that is sometimes open, sometimes not. If you hike up to the main road and take a left you'll come to a trail opposite the northern end of the bay where a 20 minute walk will take you to the 100' high *King's Bay Waterfall*. Unfortunately, if there has been little rain the falls are little more than a trickle, but if the water is flowing you can take a dip in the pool at the base of the falls. The *Tourism Office*, *TIDCO*, provides changing rooms for those inclined to take a dip in the pool.

Southwest of King's Bay is the large town of Roxborough with all the amenities. Just outside town is the multi-tiered Argyle Falls, Tobago's highest waterfall. The falls are actually in the town of Delaford on the old Rosenwald Estate. Official guides will meet you and take you on the twenty minute hike to the falls, but be sure to ask to see their badge.

From King's Bay to Scarborough, pass well offshore Queen's Island and Richmond Island to avoid inshore shoals in the vicinity of Carapuse Bay. Head for a waypoint at 11° 10.00' N, 60° 36.00' W, which places you 2 miles south of Great River Shoal as shown on Chart TOB-1. Although the better part of the shoal is quite deep, deep enough for cruising boats, the area is susceptible to rough seas and parts of it even break at times...it's best to avoid this area unless conditions and visibility permit you to venture safely closer to shore. From the waypoint south of Great River Shoal you can head for the waypoint 2 miles south of Rockly Bay and Scarborough at 11° 08.50' N, 60° 42.50' W. At this position turn to the section on Scarborough for directions on entering the harbor. Congratulations, you have just circumnavigated Tobago!

Local Cuisine

THE MULTI-CULTURAL NATURE OF TRINIDAD is nowhere more noticeable than her cuisine, a blend of African, Creole, East Indian, Amerindian, Chines, Middle Eastern, and European flavors. I don't believe there is another island in the Caribbean that offers as diverse a cross section of exotic food as Trinidad.

Everywhere you go, almost every town has a fresh fish or produce stall making it easy to find these most plentiful of resources. Kingfish is one of the most plentiful, and popular fish in Trinidad. The cascadura is a river fish that is allegedly responsible for luring Trinis back home from wherever they are. *Curry crab n' dumplin* is crab served in the shell with curry sauce and dumplings and is primarily a Tobago specialty. *Buljol*, is a blending of saltfish, onions, tomatoes, lime juice, and peppers. Served with avocado and light rolls called *hops*, *buljol* is usually served for breakfast.

While you won't be able to find it on the menu in Chaguaramas, *bush meat* is popular though hard to find. *Quenk,* the wild boar that roams the bush on Trinidad, is a very popular dish, and in the more rural areas you might find iguana, agouti, and manitou.

Today many towns in Trinidad and Tobago have fast food restaurants such as *KFC* and the local flavored favorite, *Royal Castle*. But there is a lot of street food available, and the most popular is probably the *roti,* and there are roti stands everywhere, in every small town and even the most remote hamlet. A *roti* could be considered a complete meal in a handy package. A flattened Indian bread called *dhalpourri* is filled with curried beef, chicken, shrimp, fish, or goat, along with potatoes or chick peas. The bread is folded over the filling and the creation resembles a large crepe. *Rotis* are everywhere, they're cheap, they're good, and some might be a bit hot for the unaccustomed palate. You'll find a lot of curry being used in Trinidadian dishes, (it's practically the national spice if there was such a thing) due to the huge East Indian influence. Curry is a ground blend of ginger, turmeric, fenugreek seed, cumin, coriander, fennel, pepper, cinnamon, cloves, and as many as 16–40 other herbs and spices.

Along the water's edge, especially in Maracas Bay which is famous for this, you'll find *Shark n' Bake*. A roll made from a dough that resembles a doughnut, is filled with shark (you can also get kingfish if you'd like) and deep fried. Then you have your choice of condiments to add to it and that is real treat, all sorts of hot sauces, sweet, hot, some made with mustard, some with papaya, many made with the local yellow pepper, and all tasty.

Doubles are usually breakfast and lunch snacks, though it's not improper to eat them at any time, it's just that the *doubles* shops in Port of Spain usually close after lunch. *Doubles* are very saucy, curried chick peas spread between two breads called *barahs*. You've got to be careful when eating these as they can be quite messy, and have something to drink handy as they're a tad on the hot side. *Aloo* pies are pastries filled with meat or cheese and are very popular snack though there's usually more pastry than filling. You'll often see vendors selling boiled or roasted corn on the cob, but be warned, it may be a bit tougher than you're used to. A newcomer to the fast food market in Trinidad is the Rastafarian *Ital*. Very wholesome, the rasta-inspired foods are fresh fruits and vegetables prepared with no additives and little if any salt.

Dining out in Trinidad and Tobago can be an experience in itself if you don't know what you're ordering. If you're not sure of the dish, don't be afraid to ask as people are happy to educate you in their offerings. To begin with, many places offer Creole cooking, which is primarily African and French in flavor. *Pelau* is a classic Creole dish that can have two faces. Some places serve it as a rice and peas mix, others have it as chicken based entree. Either way it consists of rice, peas, garlic, onions, mixed vegetables and in some instances cinnamon, coconut milk, and red wine. Callaloo is made from the leaves of the *dasheen* plant and is usually served as a very tasty soup though it can also be a sauce laid on rice or meat. *Mas* master Peter Minshall once made *callaloo* a theme for his *Carnival* program. *Callaloo* is often served with *Coocoo*, a creation similar to grits or polenta. Cornflour and okra are mixed, steamed with coconut milk into a cake and allowed to cool and is usually served with gravy.

Driving along the roads you're likely to see vendors selling all sorts of sweets and candies out of glass jugs called *safes*. The *Maracas Bay Scenic Overlook* on the northern coast is a good spot to sample a large selection of these wares though most towns have somebody selling them. Here you'll find safes full of coconut or currant rolls, pone (a sweet cassava bread), beer pies. Coconut sweets are prevalent, probably due to the fact that coconuts are so plentiful, and the *tooloom* is a coconut concoction that dates to slave days. The tamarind ball is a mixture of tamarind, salt, and sugar, and takes some getting used to. The *kurma* is Indian in origin. A sweet dough, the *kurma* is fried in oil until crisp and is a very popular treat in Trinidad.

Farine is a quite ordinary cereal that you can purchase in almost any market, but few know that it dates back to pre-Columbian times. The Amerindians who inhabited the islands then made the same cereal from the cassava plant, which is still popular today.

Those in search of liquid refreshment will not find Trinidad and Tobago lacking. Rum is everywhere and is very economical. Both light and dark (called "red") rums are popular here. The most popular local brands are *Vat 19* and *Old Oak* while *Royal Oak* and *Angostura Premium White* are at the upper end of the rum spectrum. Angostura is by far the most famous of the Trini produced alcoholic beverages. Angostura Bitters dates to 1824 when Dr. J.G.B. Siegert left his native Germany to assist Simon Bolivar in his fight for Venezuela independence. Bolivar's troops were plagued with stomach ailments and the good doctor began a search for a remedy. His secret formula, now know as *Angostura Bitters* is named after the Venezuelan town where Bolivar was based.

Sailors brought news of the drink to England and the beverage was first exported in 1830. The production facilities were soon moved to Trinidad where it still is today. The distillery in Laventille offers daily tours including lunch and sampling. Call Glenn Davis at 623-1841, ext. 170.

A final note on the formula that you might find interesting...so secret is the formula that only two people know the entire mix. Five people have memorized particular parts of the formula, but none of the five are allowed to travel together or even enter the blending room together, each doing his part in the process and sending it on.

Appendices

APPENDIX A: NAVIGATIONAL LIGHTS

Navigational light characteristics may differ from those published here and are subject to change without notice. It is not unusual for a light to be out of commission for long periods of time. Lights are broken down into each Island and also by area.

Trinidad-North Coast

LIGHT	CHARACTERISTICS	HT.	RNG.
Galera Point	Oc W 10s	141'	16 M
Petite Matelot Point	Fl (3) W 15s		7 M
Chupara Point	Fl (2) W 10s	325'	12 M
Saut d'Eau Island	Q W		7 M
North Post, Point a Diable	Fl W 5s	747'	14 M

Trinidad-Northwestern Tip Including Chaguaramas Bay

LIGHT	CHARACTERISTICS	HT.	RNG.
Chacachacare	Fl W 10s	825'	26 M
Chacachacare Beacon	Fl W 2s	502'	11 M
Point de Cabras	V Q (6) + L Fl W	40'	5 M
Le Chapeau Rock	Fl (3) W 10s		
Teteron Rock	Fl G 4s	24'	4 M
La Retraite Coast Guard Station	2 F R		
Gasparillo Island	Q W	36'	
Espolon Point	Fl W 4s	42'	12 M
Cronstadt Island	Q R		4 M
Reyna Point	Q G	33'	4 M
Escondida Cove	Q R	17'	
Furness-Smith Floating Dock	2 F R		
Nelson Island	Fl W 2.5s	61'	5 M
Point Sinet Range-Front	Oc W 2.5s	98'	14 M

Trinidad-Port of Spain

LIGHT	CHARACTERISTICS	HT.	RNG.
Point Sinet Range-Rear	Oc W 5s	102'	14 M
Grier Channel Range-Front 061°	Oc W 4S	135'	10 M
Grier Channel Range-Rear 061°	Iso W 2s	157'	11 M
Grier Channel #1	Fl G 3s		
Grier Channel #2	Fl R 3s		
Grier Channel #3	Q G		
Grier Channel #4	Q R		
Grier Channel #5	Q G		
Grier Channel #6	Q R		
Grier Channel #7	Fl G 5s		
Grier Channel #8	Fl R 5s		
Grier Channel #9	Q G		
Grier Channel #10	Q R		
Grier Channel #12	Q R		
Grier Channel #14	Q R		
Head of St. Vincent Jetty	F R	23'	4 M
Sea Lots Channel #1	Fl (2) G 7.5s		
Sea Lots Channel #2	V Q (9) R 10s		
Sea Lots Channel #3	Q G		
Sea Lots Channel #4	Q R		
Sea Lots Channel #5	V Q G		
Sea Lots Channel #6	V Q R		
Sea Lots Channel #7	Q G		
Sea Lots Channel #8	Q R		
Sea Lots Channel #10	L Fl R 5s		
Sea Lots Channel #12	Q R		
Sea Lots Channel #14	Q R		
Sea Lots Channel Range-Front	Oc W 10s	85'	6 M
Sea Lots Channel Range-Rear	Fl W 2s	128'	6 M

Trinidad-Point Lisas

LIGHT	CHARACTERISTICS	HT.	RNG.
Range #13-Front	Q W	30'	8 M
Range #14-Rear	Oc W 5s	52'	8 M
Marine Terminal Range-Front	Q Y	69'	10 M
Marine Terminal Range-Rear	Oc Y 3s	82'	10'
Channel Entrance #1	Fl (2) G 5s	26'	8 M
Channel Entrance #2	Fl W 3s	26'	8 M
Savonneta Range-Front	Fl W 2s	98'	8 M
Savonneta Range-Rear	Fl W 2s	135'	8 M

Trinidad-Pointe a Pierre

LIGHT	CHARACTERISTICS	HT.	RNG.
La Carriere	Fl W 2.5s	233'	23 M
Head of Pipeline Viaduct	Fl (4) W 10s	98'	14 M
Turning Basin	Fl R		
Oropuche Bank Beacon	V Q W		4 M
Brighton-Pier Front	Fl (3) W 10s	52'	15 M
Brighton-Pier Rear	Fl W 5s	100'	8 M
La Brea	Iso W 2s	26'	10 M

Trinidad-Point Fortin

LIGHT	CHARACTERISTICS	HT.	RNG.
Head of Pipeline Pier	Fl (2) W 10s	98'	14 M
North Breakwater	Fl G 3s		
South Breakwater	Fl R 3s		

Trinidad-South Coast

LIGHT	CHARACTERISTICS	HT.	RNG.
Soldado Rock	Fl w 10s		8 M
Wolf Rock	Q (6) L Fl W 15s	13'	5 M
Punta del Arenal	Fl W 7.5s	72'	16 M
Chatham Jetty	F R		3 M
Taparo Point	Fl (3) W 15s	226'	14 M
La Lune Point	Fl (4) W 20s	148'	14 M
Galeota Point	Fl W 5s	285'	16 M

Trinidad-East Coast

LIGHT	CHARACTERISTICS	HT.	RNG.
Brigand Hill	Fl (2 + 1) W 30s	712'	20 M
Tobago-North CoastSt. Giles Island	Fl W 7.5s		16 M
Man of War Bay	Q W/R/G*	82'	**
The Sisters	Fl (2) W 10s		8 M
Courland Point	L Fl W 10s		8 M
Booby Point	Fl Y 3s		4 M
Milford Bay	Q W/R/G	***	****
Crown Point	Fl (4) W 20s	115'	11 M

Tobago-South Coast

LIGHT	CHARACTERISTICS	HT.	RNG.
Little Tobago	Fl (3) W 10s	59'	5 M
Smiths Island	Fl W/R 5s*		**
Scarborough-Fort George	Fl (2) W 20s	462'	30 M
Scarborough-Range Front	ISO W/R/G***	49'	****

Tobago-South Coast (Continued)

LIGHT	CHARACTERISTICS	HT.	RNG.
Scarborough-Range Rear	Oc W 5s	66'	11 M
Bulldog Shoal	VQ (6) + L Fl 10s	16'	
Scarborough "1"	Fl G 3s	13'	4 M
Scarborough "2"	Fl R 3s	16'	5 M
Scarborough Channel East	Q R	13'	4 M
Scarborough Channel West	Fl G 3s	16'	5 M
Scarborough Breakwater	Q R	13'	5 M

TRINIDAD-EAST COAST
* White is visible 108°–131°; Red is visible 098°–108°; Green is visible 131°–141°
** White-5 M; Red-4 M; Green-4 M
*** White is visible 083°–128°; Red is visible 073°–083°; Green is visible 128°–138°
**** White-5 M; Red-4 M; Green-4 M

TOBAGO-SOUTH COAST
* White is visible 276°; Red is visible 068°–276°
** White-7 M; Red-5 M
*** White is visible 323.5°–335.5°; Red is visible 315.5°–323.5°; Green is visible 335.5°–345.5°
**** White-7M; Red-5 M; Green-5 M

APPENDIX B: GPS WAYPOINTS

Caution: GPS Waypoints are not to be used for navigational purposes. GPS waypoints are intended to place you in the general area of the described position. All routes, cuts, and anchorages must be negotiated by eyeball navigation. Waypoints do not take into account reefs and rocks between other waypoints, it is the navigator's responsibility to clear these either by heading offshore, or by passing inshore of the hazards. The author and publisher take no responsibility for the misuse of GPS waypoints. Waypoints along any tight passage offer a false sense of security and any navigator who uses waypoints to negotiate a tricky passage instead of piloting by eye is, to be blunt, a fool and deserving of whatever fate befalls him or her. Waypoints in Trinidad and Tobago are listed from north to south. Latitude is "North" and longitude is "West." Datum used is WGS84.

TRINIDAD

DESCRIPTION	N Latitude	W Longitude
Chupara Point- ½ nm NW of rock awash	10° 49.00'	61° 23.85'
Las Cuevas Bay- ½ nm NW of	10° 47.30'	61° 24.00'
Morro Point- ½ nm N of	10° 47.00'	61° 26.50'
La Vache Point- ¼ nm N of	10° 47.00'	61° 28.40'
Saut d'Eau Island- ½ nm N of	10° 46.80'	61° 30.80
La Vache Bay- ½ nm NW of	10° 46.20'	61° 29.20
Bocas del Dragon, Boca Grande- 1 nm N of	10° 43.00'	61° 46.25'
Bocas del Dragon, Boca de Navios- 1 nm N of	10° 43.00'	61° 44.35'

TRINIDAD (Continued)

DESCRIPTION	N Latitude	W Longitude
Bocas del Dragon, Boca del Huevos- 1 nm N of	10° 43.00'	61° 42.25'
Bocas del Dragon, Boca del Monos- ½ nm N of	10° 43.00'	61° 40.50'
Scotland Bay- ¼ nm SW of entrance	10° 41.75'	61° 40.20'
Carenage Bay- ¼ nm E of Alice Point and ½ nm SE of *TTSA*	10° 41.40'	61° 36.50'
Monos Island, Morris Bay- ½ nm SSE of	10° 41.40'	61° 40.20'
Monos Island, Grand Fond Bay- ½ nm SE of	10° 40.60'	61° 40.40'
Chaguaramas Bay- 1 ½ nm W of anchorage area	10° 40.50'	61° 40.00'
Chacachacare Island- ¼ nm SE of entrance to Chacachacare Bay	10° 40.40'	61° 44.00'
Cumana Bay- ¼ nm SW of TTYC	10° 40.40'	61° 34.30'
Five Islands- ¼ nm NNW of	10° 40.00'	61° 36.00'
Gaspar Grande Island- .1 nm NE of marina entrance	10° 39.80'	61° 38.90'
Gaspar Grande Island, Winns Bay- ¼ nm SW of	10° 39.55'	61° 39.65'
Port of Spain- ¼ nm SW of entrance to Grier Channel	10° 38.10'	61° 33.40'
Point-a-Pierre- ½ nm NW of entrance channel to dock	10° 20.30'	61° 29.40'

TOBAGO

DESCRIPTION	N Latitude	W Longitude
London Bridge inside passage western waypoint	11° 21.00'	60° 32.25'
London Bridge inside passage eastern waypoint	11° 21.00'	60° 31.00'
Man of War Bay- 1 nm NW of anchorage off Charlotteville	11° 20.40'	60° 34.50'
Tyrrel's Bay- 3/4 nm NE of and ½ nm N of Little Tobago Island	11° 18.90'	60° 30.40'
Parlatuvier Bay- .1 nm NW of	11° 18.23'	60° 39.30'
Englishman's Bay- ½ nm NW of anchorage area	11° 18.00'	60° 40.80'
Castara Bay- ½ nm WNW of anchorage area	11° 17.00'	60° 42.70'
King's Bay- ½ nm SE of	11° 14.90'	60° 32.60'
Great Courland Bay- ½ nm W of anchorage area	11° 12.80'	60° 47.50'
Grafton Bay (Stone Haven Bay)- ½ nm WNW of anchorage	11° 12.50'	60° 47.80'
Mt. Irvine Bay- ½ nm W of anchorage	11° 11.80'	60° 48.60'
Buccoo Bay- ¾ nm N of	11° 11.60'	60° 49.20'
Buccoo Reef- ½ nm WNW of entrance to Bon Accord Lagoon	11° 11.30'	60° 50.70'
Rockly Bay, Scarborough- ¼ nm SE of entrance channel	11° 10.35'	60° 44.05'
Pigeon Point- ½ nm W of anchorage off point	11° 10.20'	60° 51.20'
Great River Shoal- 2 miles SW of	11° 10.00'	60° 36.00'
Store Bay- ½ nm W of anchorage	11° 09.50'	60° 51.10'
Crown Point- 3 nm W of	11° 09.00'	60° 54.50'
Rockly Bay, Scarborough- 2 nm SE of and clear of Bulldog Shoal	11° 08.50'	60° 42.50'
Columbus Point- 2 nm S of	11° 06.00'	60° 47.00'

APPENDIX C: MARINAS

Some of the marinas listed below may be untenable in certain winds and dockside depths listed may not reflect entrance channel depths at low water. Always check with the Dockmaster prior to arrival. All the marinas can handle your garbage disposal problems however some may levy a charge per bag for those who are not guests at their docks. For cruisers seeking services Nearby may mean either a walk or short taxi ride away.

Trinidad

MARINA	LOCATION	FUEL	DEPTH	GROC.	DINING	E-MAIL
Bay View	Gaspar Grande	No	7'	No	Yes	
Coral Cove	Chaguaramas	No	7'	Nearby	Yes	coralcove@trinidad.net
Crews Inn	Chaguaramas	No	15'–25'	Yes	Yes	crewsinn@trinidad.net
Hummingbird	Chaguaramas	No	7'	Nearby	Yes	
Peake's	Chaguaramas	No	9'	Nearby	Yes	pys@cablenett.net
PPYC	Point-a-Pierre	Gas	6'	Nearby	Yes	
Power Boats	Chaguaramas	D & G	12'	Yes	Yes	bmfl@powerboats.co.tt
SFYC*	San Fernando	Gas	4'–6'	Nearby	Nearby	
Tardieu Marine	Chaguaramas	No	7'	Nearby	Yes	
TTYC	Bayshore	D & G	7'	Nearby	Yes	

* *The San Fernando Yacht Club* is geared primarily to shallow-draft powerboats; the waters at the dock are less than 6' at MLW, usually ranging from 6' on the outside to less than 4' further in.

APPENDIX D: SERVICE FACILITIES

As with any place, businesses come and go, sometimes seemingly overnight. Certain entries on this list may no longer exist by the time this is published. All telephone numbers are area code 868.

AUTO RENTAL

FACILITY	LOCATION	TEL. #	E-MAIL
Alfred's Rentals	Crown Point, Tobago	639-7448	
Amar Rentals, Ltd.	San Fernando, Trinidad	657-6089	
AR	Crown Point, Tobago	639-0644	
AR	Morvant, Trinidad	675-7368	

DIESEL/GENERATOR REPAIRS

FACILITY	LOCATION	TEL. #	E-MAIL
Aggreko Trinidad, Ltd.	Chaguaramas, Trinidad	665-8833	
Budget Marine	Chaguaramas, Trinidad	634-2006	sales@budmar.co.tt
Carnbee Auto & General	Carnbee, Tobago	639-9304	
Dockyard Electric (Crews Inn)	Chaguaramas, Trinidad	634-4272	dockelec@trinida.net

DIESEL/GENERATOR REPAIRS (Continued)

FACILITY	LOCATION	TEL. #	E-MAIL
Engines Engines (Tardieu)	Chaguaramas, Trinidad	634-1164	
Engine Tech	Arima, Trinidad	667-7158	
General Diesel	La Romain, Trinidad	652-5441	
General Diesel	San Fernando, Trinidad	657-6351	
Gitten's Engine (Tardieu)	Chaguaramas, Trinidad	634-2304	adian@tstt.net.tt
JN Marine Sales & Service	Lowlands, Tobago	639-0233	
L & P Marine Supplies	Pt. Cumana, Trinidad	633-3395	lmarine@opus.co.tt
L & P Marine Supplies	Chaguaramas, Trinidad	634-2094	lmarine@opus.co.tt
L & W Marine Engines	Laventille, Trinidad	624-5618	
Laughlin & Degannes	Port of Spain, Trinidad	625-1712	
Tracmac	Chaguaramas, Trinidad	665-5555	
Trinidad Detroit (Cor. C.)	Chaguaramas, Trinidad	634-2177	
Trintrac	Chase Village, Trinidad	672-5329	trintrac@caribsurf.net
Tropical Power	Chaguaramas, Trinidad	665-8833	

ELECTRONICS/ELECTRICAL

FACILITY	LOCATION	TEL. #	E-MAIL
Boyce Electronics	Marabella, Trinidad	658-2943	
Budget Marine	Chaguaramas, Trinidad	634-2006	sales@budmar.co.tt
Carib. Marine (Power Boats)	Chaguaramas, Trinidad	634-4561	electromarine@trinidad.net
Tang Yuk (Coral Cove)	Chaguaramas, Trinidad	634-2279	tye@trinidad.net
Dockyard El. (Crews Inn)	Chaguaramas, Trinidad	634-4272	dockelec@trinida.net
Echo Marine	Chaguaramas, Trinidad	634-2027	sailfly@trinidad.net
Electropics Marine Service	Chaguaramas, Trinidad	634-2322	electrop@tstt.net.tt
Goodwood Mar. (Crews Inn)	Chaguaramas, Trinidad	634-2203	goodwood@tstt.net.tt
L & P Marine Supplies	Point Cumana, Trinidad	633-3395	lmarine@opus.co.tt
L & P Marine Supplies	Chaguaramas, Trinidad	634-2094	lmarine@opus.co.tt
Navtech (Coral Cove)	Chaguaramas, Trinidad	653-8602	
Peake Chandlery	Chaguaramas, Trinidad	634-4006	
Peake Thomas & Co.	Cocorite, Trinidad	622-8816	
Serge Electrical (Peake's)	Chaguaramas, Trinidad	634-4420	
Solar Power Systems	Laventille, Trinidad	624-2665	climate@tstt.net.tt
Stuart Electronics	Chaguaramas, Trinidad	634-1164	stutron@tstt.net.tt

FABRICATION/WELDING

FACILITY	LOCATION	TEL. #	E-MAIL
AK Engineering	Tunapuna, Trinidad	663-9776	
Ali's Mach. (Power Boats)	Chaguaramas, Trinidad	634-4420	
Atlantic Yacht Services	Chaguaramas, Trinidad	634-4337	
Caribbean Welders (IMS)	Chaguaramas, Trinidad	634-1074	
Chag. Metal (Tardieu)	Chaguaramas, Trinidad	631-1164	
Degannes (Power Boats)	Chaguaramas, Trinidad	634-4025	
Eddo's Welding	San Fernando, Trinidad	662-2027	

FABRICATION/WELDING (Continued)

FACILITY	LOCATION	TEL. #	E-MAIL
Francis Marine	Crown Point, Tobago		
Gormandy's Engineering	Trinidad	623-6661	
Speedway Auto & Mach.	Lambeau Village, Tobago	639-3802	

HAUL OUT

FACILITY	LOCATION	TEL. #	E-MAIL
Coral Cove Marina	Chaguaramas, Trinidad	634-2040	coralcove@trinidad.net
Crews Inn Marina	Chaguaramas, Trinidad	634-4828	crewsinn@tstt.net.tt
IMS Yacht Services	Chaguaramas, Trinidad	625-2104	ims@imsyacht.com
Peake Yacht Services	Chaguaramas, Trinidad	634-4420	pys@cablenett.net
Power Boats	Chaguaramas, Trinidad	634-4303	bmfl@powerboats.co.tt
TTSA	Carenage, Trinidad	634-4519	

HOSPITALS

FACILITY	LOCATION	TEL. #	E-MAIL
Arima District Hospital	Arima, Trinidad	667-3503	
Community Hospital	Port of Spain, Trinidad	622-1191	
Mount Hope	St. Augustine, Trinidad	662-3552	
Port of Spain General	Port of Spain, Trinidad	623-2951	
San Fernando General	San Fernando, Trinidad	658-3581	
St. Clair Med. Cntr.	Port of Spain, Trinidad	628-1451	
Tobago County Hospital	Scarborough, Tobago	639-2551	

HULL REPAIR/PAINT

FACILITY	LOCATION	TEL. #	E-MAIL
Coral Cove Marina	Chaguaramas, Trinidad	634-2040	coralcove@trinidad.net
Crews Inn Marina	Chaguaramas, Trinidad	634-4828	crewsinn@tstt.net.tt
IMS Yacht Services	Chaguaramas, Trinidad	625-2104	ims@imsyacht.com
Francois (Peake's)	Chaguaramas, Trinidad	634-2066	
Peake Yacht Services	Chaguaramas, Trinidad	634-4420	pys@cablenett.net
Power Boats	Chaguaramas, Trinidad	634-4303	bmfl@powerboats.co.tt
Rainbow (Power Boats)	Chaguaramas, Trinidad	646-5020	

INFLATABLES/LIFERAFTS

FACILITY	LOCATION	TEL. #	E-MAIL
Budget Marine	Chaguaramas, Trinidad	634-2006	sales@budmar.co.tt
Echo Marine	Chaguaramas, Trinidad	634-2027	sailfly@trinidad.net
Marine Consultants	Port of Spain, Trinidad	625-2887	
Marine Safety Equipment	Chaguaramas, Trinidad	634-4410	
Power Boats	Chaguaramas, Trinidad	634-4303	bmfl@powerboats.co.tt
Survival Systems	Port of Spain, Trinidad	659-1680	
TTSA	Carenage, Trinidad	634-4519	

INTERNET ACCESS

FACILITY	LOCATION	TEL. #	E-MAIL
Blue Waters Inn	Anse Bateau, Tobago	660-2583	bwi@bluwatersinn.com
Charlotteville Beach Bar	Crown Point, Tobago		
Clothes Wash Cafe	Crown Point, Tobago	639-0007	
Cyber Cafe	Crown Point, Tobago	639-7461	sunfun@trinidad.net
Cyber Sea (Coral Cove)	Chaguaramas, Trinidad		
Island Surf Cafe (IMS)	Chaguaramas, Trinidad	634-2407	islandsurfcafe@chaguaramas.com
Jupiter Tech	Scarborough, Tobago		
Mariners Off. (Crews Inn)	Chaguaramas, Trinidad	634-4183	mariner@tstt.net.tt
Matrix Technology	Scarborough, Trinidad	639-4220	matrixtechnology@tstt.net.tt
Netsurf (ITC at Starlite)	Diego Martin, Trinidad	627-1246	
Ocean Internet (Peake's)	Chaguaramas, Trinidad	634-1038	oceaninternet@yahoo.co.uk
Ocean Internet (Pwr Bts.)	Chaguaramas, Trinidad	634-1205	oceaninternet@yahoo.co.uk
Ocean Internet (Tardieu)	Chaguaramas, Trinidad	634-2233	oceaninternet@yahoo.co.uk
Original Pancake House	Crown Point, Tobago	639-9866	
Public Library (free)	Charlotteville, Tobago		
Public Library (free)	Scarborough, Tobago		
SameS@me	Chaguaramas, Trinidad	634-1360	samesame@whoever.com
Shenda's Email	Charlotteville, Tobago		
Tourism Office (airport)	Crown Point, Tobago	639-2125	tourbago@tstt.net

MARINE SUPPLIES

FACILITY	LOCATION	TEL. #	E-MAIL
Anchorage Ship Chand.	Port of Spain, Trinidad	623-7979	
Boat Shop #1	Glencoe, Trinidad	637-2628	
Boat Shop #2	Chaguaramas, Trinidad	634-4148	
Boater's Shop (Pwr.Bts.)	Chaguaramas, Trinidad	634-4303	
Budget Marine	Chaguaramas, Trinidad	634-2006	sales@budmar.co.tt
Caribbean Marine	Chaguaramas, Trinidad	634-4561	
Caribbean Safety	Point Lisas, Trinidad	636-1732	
Corsa Marine (Tardieu)	Chaguaramas, Trinidad	634-1054	
Corsa Marine	San Fernando, Trinidad	657-4880	
Corsa Marine	Bon Accord, Tobago	639-2628	
Crews Inn Boatyard	Chaguaramas, Trinidad	634-4384	
Echo Marine	Chaguaramas, Trinidad	634-2027	sailfly@trinidad.net
Elee Agencies	Port of Spain, Trinidad	633-2221	
Engine Tech	Arima, Trinidad	667-7158	
Eswil (Mariner's Haven)	Chaguaramas, Trinidad	634-2327	
Goodwood Marine	Goodwood Park, Trinidad	632-4612	
Marine Warehouse	Chaguaramas, Trinidad	634-4150	tiems@tstt.net.tt
L & P Marine Supplies	Pt. Cumana, Trinidad	633-3395	lmarine@opus.co.tt
L & P Marine Supplies	Chaguaramas, Trinidad	634-2094	lmarine@opus.co.tt
L & W Marine Engines	Laventille, Trinidad	624-5618	

MARINE SUPPLIES (Continued)

FACILITY	LOCATION	TEL. #	E-MAIL
Marc One	Chaguaramas, Trinidad	634-2259	
Marine Consultants	Port of Spain, Trinidad	625-1309	
Mariner Outboards	Crown Point, Tobago	639-1170	
Maska	San Fernando, Trinidad	653-3912	
Peake Chandlery	Chaguaramas, Trinidad	634-4006	peakechn@carib-link.net
Peake Chandlery	Cocorite, Trinidad	622-8816	peakechn@carib-link.net
Power Boats	Chaguaramas, Trinidad	634-4303	pbmfl@powerboats.co.tt
Shakeer & Sons	Chaguanas, Trinidad	665-8119	
Trinidad Ropework	Port of Spain, Trinidad	642-3146	
West Point Auto & Mar.	Carenage, Trinidad	633-2625	

SAIL/CANVAS REPAIR

FACILITY	LOCATION	TEL. #	E-MAIL
Ace Sails (Coral Cove)	Chaguaramas, Trinidad	634-1521	info@DrawTheACE.com
Alpha Canvas (Tardieu)	Chaguaramas, Trinidad	683-1713	alphacanvas@hotmail.com
Barrow Sails & Canvas	Chaguaramas, Trinidad	634-4137	barrow@tstt.net.tt
Calypso Canvas (Peake's)	Chaguaramas, Trinidad	634-4012	
Calypso Mar. Canvas	Chaguaramas, Trinidad	633-8709	
Canvas Works	Chaguaramas, Trinidad	632-4059	
Frankie's Upholstery	San Fernando, Trinidad	679-3925	
KNJ Marine (Peake's)	Chaguaramas, Trinidad	634-1021	knjm@cablenett.net
Ocean Sails (IMS)	Chaguaramas, Trinidad	634-4560	
Soca Sails (Crews Inn)	Chaguaramas, Trinidad	634-4178	info@socasails.com
Upholstery Shop (PB)	Chaguaramas, Trinidad	634-4134	
Webster's Can. (Tardieu)	Chaguaramas, Trinidad		

APPENDIX E: LOGARITHMIC SPEED SCALE

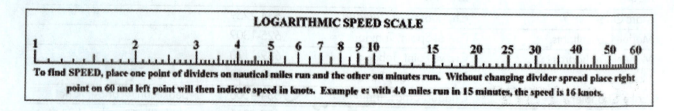

APPENDIX F: DEPTH CONVERSION SCALE

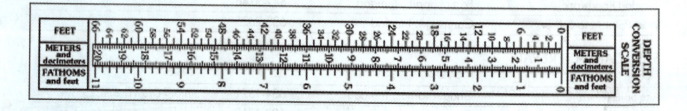

APPENDIX G: METRIC CONVERSION TABLE

Visitors to the Eastern Caribbean, and Trinidad and Tobago in particular, will find the metric system in use and many grocery items, roadway mileage signs, and fuel measures will be metric. As a rule of thumb, a meter is just a little longer than a yard and a liter is very close to a quart. If in doubt, use the following table.

1 centimeter (cm) = 0.4 inch	1 inch = 2.54 cm
1 meter (m) = 3.28 feet	1 foot = 0.31 cm
1 m = 0.55 fathoms	1 fathom = 1.83 m
1 kilometer (km) = 0.62 NM	1 yard = 0.93 m
1 km = 0.54 nautical NM	1 nautical mile = 1.852 km
1 liter (l) = 0.26 gallons	1 gallon = 3.75 l
1 gram (g) = 0.035 ounce	1 ounce = 28.4 g
1 metric ton (t) = 1.1 tons U.S.	1 pound = 454 g

References
(and Suggested Reading)

A Cruising Guide to the Caribbean and the Bahamas; Jerrems C. Hart and William T. Stone, Dodd, Mead and Company, New York, 1982

A Cruising Guide to the Exumas Cays Land and Sea Park; Stephen J. Pavlidis with Ray Darville, Night Flyer Enterprises, U.S.A., 1994

A History of Modern Trinidad, 1783–1962; B. Bereton, Heinnemann Pub., U.S./U.K.

American Practical Navigator; Nathaniel Bowditch, LL.D., DMA Hydrographic Center, 1977

A Preliminary Study of the Buccoo Reef/Bon Accord Complex; J.S. Kenny, UWI, TT, 1976

Best Dives of the Caribbean; Joyce and Jon Huber, Hunter Publishing, Edison, NJ, 1998

Cote ce Cote la, Trinidad and Tobago Dictionary; John Mendes, College Press, Trinidad, 1986

David Frost Introduces Trinidad and Tobago; Andre Deutsch, Ltd., 1975

Insight Guides, Trinidad and Tobago; APA Productions, Ltd., 1987

On and Off the Beaten Path, The Central and Southern Bahamas Guide; Stephen J. Pavlidis, Seaworthy Publications, Inc., Port Washington, WI., 2002

Sailing Directions for the Caribbean Sea; Pub. #147, Defense Mapping Agency, #SDPUB147

Spanish Trinidad; C.R. Ottley, Longman Pub., U.K.

The Abaco Guide; Stephen J. Pavlidis, Seaworthy Publications, Inc., Port Washington, WI., 2002

The Concise Guide to Caribbean Weather; David Jones, 1996

The Exuma Guide, 2nd Edition; Stephen J. Pavlidis, Seaworthy Publications, Inc., Port Washington WI., 2002

The Ocean Almanac; Robert Hendrickson, Doubleday, New York, 1984

The Story of Tobago; C.R. Ottley, Longman Pub., U.K.

The Tainos; Irving Rouse, Yale University Press, New Haven and London, 1992

The Turks and Caicos Guide, 2nd Edition; Stephen J. Pavlidis, Seaworthy Publications, Inc., Port Washington, WI., 2002

Index

A

Adventure Farm and Nature Reserve 84
Airport 75
Alcatras Point 34
Alice Point 47, 48
Anse Bateau 93, 94, 107
Anse Brisant 93, 94
Arawaks 3
Argyle Falls 96
Arima 9, 54, 65, 66, 69, 105–107
Arnos Vale 15, 84
Arnos Vale Bay 84
Arnos Vale Waterwheel 84
Asa Wright Nature Center 34, 65, 66
Avocat Falls 66

B

Back Bay 80
Bacolet 74
Balata Bay 62, 64
Bande du Sud 38, 40
Barrel of Beef 81–83
Begorrat Island 49
Belmont Bay 93
Belmont Reef 93
Bird of Paradise Island 93, 94
Black Rock 80–82, 92, 93
Blanchette Point 35, 36
Blanchisseuse 34, 60, 65
Blind Passage 77
Bloody Bay 32, 71, 89
Boca de Huevos 33, 35
Boca de Monos 33–36, 41, 61
Boca de Navios 33, 35, 39
Boca del Dragon 33, 37
Boca del Serpiente 34, 67
Boca Grande 35, 102
Boca Sin Entrada 37
Bocas del Dragon 25, 33, 102, 103
Bocas, the 17, 25

Bolo Rocks 35, 40
Bombshell Bay 45, 47, 48
Bon Accord 74, 76, 78, 103, 107
Bon Accord Lagoon 75, 77, 78, 103
Booby Point 80, 101
Booby Reef 89, 91
Botanical Gardens 56, 74
Brasso Seco 66
Brothers, the 71, 89, 90
Buccoo 20, 74, 78, 79
Buccoo Bay 76–79, 103
Buccoo Point 77
Buccoo Reef 15, 32, 71, 75–78, 103
Buccoo Reef National Park 78
Bulldog Shoal 71, 72, 102, 103
Bush Bush Sanctuary 69

C

Caledonia Island 47, 49
Calypso Tents 10
Cambleton 89, 91
Cambleton Battery 89, 91
Cambleton Bay 89, 90
Cangrejos Point 34
Cannings Point 35, 41, 42, 49
Capital of the South 58
Carapuse Bay 71, 96
Cardinal Reef 89, 91
Cardinal Rock 89
Carenage 7, 9, 18, 40–42, 47–50, 54, 106, 108
Carenage Bay 42, 47, 48, 50, 103
Caribbean Etiquette 12
CARICOM 8
Carnival 8–12, 20, 22, 25, 54, 56, 64, 70, 98
Caroni Swamp 16, 34, 55, 56
Carrera Island 47, 48, 49
Castara 85, 86
Castara Bay 32, 71, 85, 86, 103
Castara River 86
Cedros 67
Cedros Bay 34

Cedros Point 34
Centipede Island 42
Centipede Point 41
Chacachacare 7, 8, 18, 33–40, 99, 103
Chaguanas 24, 34, 55–57, 108
Chaguaramas 6, 8, 9, 11, 14, 15, 17, 18, 20, 22–27, 33, 34, 39–44, 49–51, 53–56, 61, 69, 76, 97, 99, 103–108
Chaguaramas Bay 6, 8, 14, 18, 25, 26, 33, 36, 40–44, 47, 49–51
Chaguaramas Hotel and Convention Center 8, 22, 51
Chaguaramas Military History and Aviation Museum 51
Charlotteville 14, 21, 22, 32, 71, 87, 89–92, 96, 103, 107
Chupara Point 34, 65, 68, 71, 99, 102
Citygate 55
Cocal 17, 69
Cocal, The 34
Cocorite 108
Cocorite Bay 47
Cocos Bay 34
Columbus Channel 3, 34
Columbus Point 71, 72, 103
Corozal Point 34
Corral Point 34
Courland Monument 82
Courland Point 81–83, 101
Craig Island 47
Creteau 49
Cronstadt Island 47–49, 99
Crown Point 15, 19, 22, 32, 71–76, 79, 101–104, 106–108
Culloden Bay 15, 71, 83, 84
Culture 12
Cumana Bay 47, 51, 103
Curao Point 34
Currency 13
Customs and Immigration 14
Cyril's Bay 60, 62

D

Deep Channel 77
Delaford 95, 96
Delgada Point 42
Devil's Woodyard 68
Diego Islands 47–50
Diego Martin 107
Diego Martin Islands 49
Diving 15
Dominique Point 35, 36

E

Education 15
Emperor Valley Zoo 56
Englishman's Bay 32, 71, 86, 87, 90, 103
Englishman's Bay State Nature Reserve 86
Erin Bay 34
Erin Point 34
Escondida Cove 99
Espolon Point 99

F

False Channel 77, 78
Ferries 16
Ferry Terminal 14, 19, 72, 73
Five Islands 7, 47, 49, 50, 61, 103
Flagstaff Hill 91
Fort Apodaca 47
Fort Bennet 80, 81
Fort Chacon 56
Fort George 56, 72, 74, 101
Fort James 82
Fort King George 73, 74
Fort Milford 76
Fort Picton 56
Fort St. Andres, 56

G

Galeota Point 34, 101
Galera Point 34, 71, 99
Galleon Passage 71
Gaspar Grande 34, 35, 47–49, 104
Gaspar Grande Island 41, 45–51, 103
Gasparee 41, 47, 48
Gasparillo Island 41, 42, 47, 99
Gasparillo Point 41
Gibson Channel 77, 78
Gilpin Trace 87
Goat Island 15, 93–95
Godineau River 66
Goodwood Park 107
Grafton Bay 79, 80, 82, 103
Grafton Caledonia Wildlife Sanctuary 80
Grand Courland Bay 82
Grand Fond Bay 35, 36, 103
Grande Riviere Bay 34
Great Courland Bay 15, 32, 71, 81–85, 103
Great Fond Bay 36
Great River Shoal 71, 96, 103
Grier Channel 52, 54, 55
Guayaguayare 7, 17, 34, 68, 69
Guayaguayare Bay 34
Gulf of Paria 4–6, 16, 21, 25, 33, 39, 54, 61, 66, 67, 69

H

howler monkeys 36, 37, 69
Huevos Island 17, 33, 35, 37, 39
hurricanes 21, 22

I

Icacos 26, 66, 67
Independence Square 19, 55
Indian Walk 3
Isla Margarita 16
Isolete Bay 34
Isolete Point 34

J

J'Ouvert 11, 54

K

Kariwak Reef 75
Ketchup Reef 75, 77
Kethcup Reef 77
Kimmee Museum 80
King's Bay 32, 71, 72, 95, 96, 103

L

La Brea 7, 34, 66, 67, 101
La Carriere 101
La Fillete Bay 65
La Lune Point 101
La Trinta Bay 35, 37, 38
La Vache 63
La Vache Bay 60–64, 102
La Vache Point 60, 62, 64, 102
Lampsinburgh 72, 73
L'Anse Fourmi 87
Las Cuevas 64, 65
Las Cuevas Bay 64, 102
Laventille 55, 56, 105
Le Chapeau 34, 35, 99
Les Boquets Islands 60, 62
Les Couteaux 85
les remous 25
Little Tobago 71, 101
Little Tobago Island 15, 93–95, 103
Little Tobago Reef 95
London Bridge 15, 32, 71, 92, 94, 103
Long Islands 49
Long Rock 93, 94
Los Gallos Point 34

M

Macqueripe Bay 34, 61
Magnetic Road 64
Magnificent Seven 56
Mal d'Estomac 60, 62
Man of War 89
Man of War Bay 71, 89–91, 101, 103
Manchineel trees 40
Manzanilla 69
Manzilla Point 34
Marabella 105
Maracas 64
Maracas Bay 34, 62–64, 71
Maracas Waterfall 64
Marble Island 92
Margarita 4, 23, 24, 27
mas 11
Mason Hall 74
Masson Bay 48, 50
Matelot 34, 65, 99
Matura Bay 34
Mayaro 34, 67, 69
Mayaro Bay 34
Medine Point 60, 62
Melville Islands 92, 94
Milford Bay 74, 77, 101
Milford Road 76
Minshall, Peter 11
Monos Island 33–37, 103
Morne la Croix 66
Morris Bay 35, 36, 103
Morro Point 62, 102
Moruga 3, 34, 68
Moruga Point 34
Mount Catherine 41
Mount El Tucuche 60, 64, 65
Mt. Irvine 74, 79
Mt. Irvine Bay 79, 80, 103
Mt. Irvine Reef 80
Mt. Pleasant 74, 79
mud volcanoes 68

N

Narvia Swamp 34, 69
Negra Point 34
Neilson's Island 49
Nelson Island 7, 47, 49, 50, 61, 99
No Man's Land 78
Nylon Pool 77–79

O

Oropuche Lagoon 34, 66
Oropuche River 66

P

Palo Seco 7, 34
Palo Seco Bay 34

Paria Bay 34
Parlatuvier 87, 88
Parlatuvier Bay 86–89, 103
Patience Hill 79
Pelican Island 47, 50
Peter Minshall 11
Petite Matelot Point 99
Pierreville 69
Pigeon Point 74, 75, 77, 78, 103
Pigeon Point Reef 75
Pigeon Point Resort 75, 77
Piparo 68
Pirates Bay 90, 91
Pirates Reef 90
Pitch Lake 66, 67
Plaisance 69
Pleasant Prospect 81
Plymouth 5, 72, 81–84
Point a Diable 99
Point Baleine 47–49
Point Cumana 105
Point de Cabras 99
Point Delgada 41, 42
Point Fortin 34
Point Gourde 41, 47–51
Point Lisas 34, 58, 100, 107
Point Radix 34
Point-a-Pierre 7, 34, 57, 58, 103, 104
Pointed Rock 92, 94
Port of Spain 4–6, 8, 10–12, 15, 16, 34, 47, 52–59, 61, 62, 64–66, 69, 72, 100, 103, 105–108
PPYC 57, 58, 104
Princes Town 3, 4, 67, 68
Princess Town 34

Q

Queen's Bay 71
Queen's Island 96
Queen's Park Savannah 56, 61
Quinam Bay 67

R

Reyna Point 99
Richmond Island 71, 96
Rio Claro 34, 68, 69
Rock Island 50
Rockly Bay 72–74, 96, 103
Rocky Point 79, 80
Roja Point 34
Roxborough 87, 91, 96

S

Saline Bay 34
San Fernando 34, 55, 58–60, 66, 67, 104–108
Sanders Bay 40
Sangre Grande 34, 66, 69
Saut d'Eau Island 34, 60, 62, 99, 102
Savanna Grande 3, 4, 68
Scarborough 71–74, 76, 89, 91, 96, 106, 107
Scotland Bay 36
Sea Lots Channel 52, 55, 100
SFYC 59, 104
Signal Hill 79
Siparia 7, 34, 67
Sisters, the 15, 39, 71, 89, 90, 101
South Quay 56
Speyside 71, 92, 94, 95
St. Augustine 106
St. Giles Island 71, 92, 94, 101
St. James 55
St. Joseph 4, 6, 34, 64
St. Vincent Jetty 52, 54, 100
Stanislas Bay 38, 40
Staubles Bay 41
Stone Haven Bay 80
Store Bay 74–76, 78, 103

T

Taparo Point 101
Teteron Bay 35, 36, 42
Teteron Rock 35, 36, 42, 49, 99
The Brothers 71, 89, 90
The Sisters 15, 39, 71, 89, 90, 101
Tobago Forest Reserve 87
Toco 4, 34, 65
Trinity Hills Wildlife Sanctuary 69
TTSA 9, 41, 42, 49, 50, 103
TTYC 40, 42, 51, 53–55, 103, 104
Turning Basin 101
Tyrrel's Bay 71, 92–95, 103

V

VAT (Value Added Tax) 13

W

Wasp Shoal 72, 74
Weather Rocks 93–95
Westmoorings Mall 54, 55
Winn's Bay 48

Y

Yarra River 65
YSATT 27, 28, 42, 43

About the Author

Stephen J. Pavlidis has been cruising and living aboard his 40' sloop *IV Play* since the winter of 1989. Starting in the Exuma Cays, over a decade ago, Steve began a career writing guides to the many fascinating destinations he visited. Many of his books stand alone to this day as the quintessential guides to the areas he covers. His books are different than most other cruising guides in some very significant ways. All of the charts in Steve's books were created using data personally collected while visiting each area using a computerized system that interfaces DGPS and depth soundings. The result are charts so accurate that they are utilized by SoftChart International, a leading provider of digital charts and navigation data, to provide additional detail that supplements government produced charts.

So far in his career, Steve has written a set of four guides covering the entire Bahamas/Turks and Caicos region including *The Exuma Guide, On and Off the Beaten Path, A Guide to the Central and Southern Bahamas, The Turks and Caicos Guide,* and *The Abaco Guide.*

A Cruising Guide to Puerto Rico, including the Spanish Virgin Islands and *A Cruising Guide to Trinidad and Tobago* begin the next phase of Pavlidis' books covering the entire Caribbean. These two releases will be followed by guides covering the Windward, Leeward, and Virgin Islands. You can find out more about this exceptional author by visiting his Web site http://www.islandhopping.com where there is current news, information about Steve's lastest projects, and contact information.

Notes